The Girl from the Marsh Croft

Selma Lagerlöf

BIBLIOBAZAAR

The Girl
From the Marsh Croft

By Selma Lagerlöf

Author of " The Story of Gösta Berling," " The
Miracles of Antichrist," " Invisible Links," etc.

Translated from the Swedish

By Velma Swanston Howard

Boston
Little, Brown, and Company
1910

PREFATORY NOTE

READERS of Miss Lagerlöf will observe that in this, her latest book, "The Girl from the Marsh Croft," the Swedish author has abandoned her former world of Romanticism and has entered the field of Naturalism and Realism.

This writer's romantic style is most marked, perhaps, in her first successful work, "Gösta Berling."

How "The Story of Gösta Berling" grew, and the years required to perfect it, is told in the author's unique literary autobiography, "The Story of a Story," which is embodied in the present volume.

In "The Girl from the Marsh Croft" Miss Lagerlöf has courageously chosen a girl who had gone astray as the heroine of her love story, making her innate honesty and goodness the redemptive qualities which win for her the love of an honest man and the respect and esteem of all.

To the kindness of the publishers of *Good Housekeeping*, I am indebted for permission to include " The Legend of the Christmas Rose " in this volume.

This book is translated and published with the sanction of the author, Selma Lagerlöf.

CONTENTS

The Girl from the Marsh Croft

The Girl from the Black Cove

The Girl from the
Marsh Croft

I

IT took place in the court room of a rural district. At the head of the Judges' table sits an old Judge — a tall and massively built man, with a broad, rough-hewn visage. For several hours he has been engaged in deciding one case after another, and finally something like disgust and melancholy has taken hold of him. It is difficult to know if it is the heat and closeness of the court room that are torturing him or if he has become low-spirited from handling all these petty wrangles, which seem to spring from no other cause than to bear witness to people's quarrel-mania, uncharitableness, and greed.

He has just begun on one of the last cases to be tried during the day. It concerns a plea for help in the rearing of a child.

This case had already been tried at the last Court Session, and the protocols of the former suit are being read; therefore one learns that

the plaintiff is a poor farmer's daughter and the
defendant is a married man.

Moreover, it says in the protocol, the defendant maintains that the plaintiff has wrongfully,
unjustly, and only with the desire of profiting
thereby, sued the defendant. He admits that
at one time the plaintiff had been employed in
his household, but that during her stay in his
home he had not carried on any intrigue with
her, and she has no right to demand assistance
from him. The plaintiff still holds firmly to her
claim, and after a few witnesses have been heard,
the defendant is called to take the oath and
show cause why he should not be sentenced by
the Court to assist the plaintiff.

Both parties have come up and are standing,
side by side, before the Judges' table. The
plaintiff is very young and looks frightened to
death. She is weeping from shyness and with
difficulty wipes away the tears with a crumpled
handkerchief, which she does n't seem to know
how to open out. She wears black clothes,
which are quite new and whole, but they fit so
badly that one is tempted to think she has borrowed them in order to appear before the Court
of Justice in a befitting manner.

As regards the defendant, one sees at a glance
that he is a prosperous man. He is about

forty and has a bold and dashing appearance. As he stands before the Court, he has a very good bearing. One can see that he does not think it a pleasure to stand there, but he does n't appear to be the least concerned about it.

As soon as the protocols have been read, the Judge turns to the defendant and asks him if he holds fast to his denials and if he is prepared to take the oath.

To these questions the defendant promptly answers a curt yes. He digs down in his vest pocket and takes out a statement from the clergyman who attests that he understands the meaning and import of the oath and is qualified to take it.

All through this the plaintiff has been weeping. She appears to be unconquerably bashful, and doggedly keeps her eyes fixed upon the floor. Thus far she has not raised her eyes sufficiently to look the defendant in the face.

As he utters his " yes," she starts back. She moves a step or two nearer the Court, as if she had something to say to the contrary, and then she stands there perplexed. It is hardly possible, she seems to say to herself; he cannot have answered yes. I have heard wrongly.

Meanwhile the Judge takes the clergyman's paper and motions to the court officer. The latter goes up to the table to find the Bible, which lies hidden under a pile of records, and lays it down in front of the defendant.

The plaintiff hears that some one is walking past her and becomes restless. She forces herself to raise her eyes just enough to cast a glance over the table, and she sees then how the court officer moves the Bible.

Again it appears as though she wished to raise some objection, and again she controls herself. It is n't possible that he will be allowed to take the oath. Surely the Judge must prevent him!

The Judge is a wise man and knows how people in her home district think and feel. He knew, very likely, how severe all people were as soon as there was anything which affected the marriage relation. They knew of no worse sin than the one she had committed. Would she ever have confessed anything like this about herself if it were not true? The Judge must understand the awful contempt that she had brought down upon herself, and not contempt only, but all sorts of misery. No one wanted her in service — no one wanted her work. Her own parents could scarcely tolerate her presence in their cabin and talked all the while of casting her out. Oh, the Judge must know that she would never have asked for help from a married man had she no right to it.

Surely the Judge could not believe that she lied in a case like this; that she would have called down upon herself such a terrible misfortune if she had had any one else to accuse than a married man. And if he knows this, he must stop the oath-taking.

She sees that the Judge reads through the clergyman's statements a couple of times and she begins to think he intends to interfere.

True, the Judge has a wary look. Now he shifts his glance to the plaintiff, and with that his weariness and disgust become even more marked. It appears as though he were unfavorably disposed toward her. Even if the plaintiff is telling the truth, she is nevertheless a bad woman and the Judge cannot feel any sympathy for her.

Sometimes the Judge interposes in a case, like a good and wise counsellor, and keeps the parties from ruining themselves entirely. But to-day he is tired and cross and thinks only of letting the legal process have its course.

He lays down the clergyman's recommendation and says a few words to the defendant to the effect that he hopes he has carefully considered the consequences of a perjured oath.

The defendant listens to him with the calm air which he has shown all the while, and he answers respectfully and not without dignity.

The plaintiff listens to this in extreme terror She makes a few vehement protests and wrings her hands. Now she wants to speak to the Court. She struggles frightfully with her shyness and with the sobs which prevent her speaking. The result is that she cannot get out an audible word.

Then the oath will be taken! She must give it up. No one will prevent him from swearing away his soul.

Until now, she could not believe this possible. But now she is seized with the certainty that it is close at hand — that it will occur the next second. A fear more overpowering than any she has hitherto felt takes possession of her. She is absolutely paralyzed. She does not even weep more. Her eyes are glazed. It is his intention, then, to bring down upon himself eternal punishment.

She comprehends that he wants to swear himself free for the sake of his wife. But even if the truth were to make trouble in his home, he should not for that reason throw away his soul's salvation.

There is nothing so terrible as perjury. There

is something uncanny and awful about that sin.
There is no mercy or condonation for it. The
gates of the infernal regions open of their own
accord when the perjurer's name is mentioned.

If she had then raised her eyes to his face, she
would have been afraid of seeing it stamped with
damnation's mark, branded by the wrath of God.

As she stands there and works herself into
greater and greater terror, the Judge instructs
the defendant as to how he must place his fingers
on the Bible. Then the Judge opens the law
book to find the form of the oath.

As she sees him place his fingers on the book,
she comes a step nearer, and it appears as though
she wished to reach across the table and push
his hand away.

But as yet she is restrained by a faint hope.
She thinks he will relent now — at the last
moment.

The Judge has found the place in the law book,
and now he begins to administer the oath loudly
and distinctly. Then he makes a pause for the
defendant to repeat his words. The defendant
actually starts to repeat, but he stumbles over
the words, and the Judge must begin again
from the beginning.

Now she can no longer entertain a trace of
hope. She knows now that he means to swear

falsely — that he means to bring down upon himself the wrath of God, both for this life and for the life to come.

She stands wringing her hands in her helplessness. And it is all her fault because she has accused him! But she was without work; she was starving and freezing; the child came near dying. To whom else should she turn for help? Never had she thought that he would be willing to commit such an execrable sin.

The Judge has again administered the oath. In a few seconds the thing will have been done: the kind of thing from which there is no turning back — which can never be retrieved, never blotted out.

Just as the defendant begins to repeat the oath, she rushes forward, sweeps away his outstretched hand, and seizes the Bible.

It is her terrible dread which has finally given her courage. He must not swear away his soul; he must not!

The court officer hastens forward instantly to take the Bible from her and to bring her to order. She has a boundless fear of all that pertains to a Court of Justice and actually believes that what she has just done will bring her to prison; but she does not let go her hold on the Bible. Cost what it may, he cannot take the oath. He who would swear also runs up to take the Bible, but she resists him too.

"You shall not take the oath!" she cries, "you shall not!"

That which is happening naturally awakens the greatest surprise. The court attendants elbow their way up to the bar, the jurymen start to rise, the recording clerk jumps up with the ink bottle in his hand to prevent its being upset.

Then the Judge shouts in a loud and angry tone, "Silence!" and everybody stands perfectly still.

"What is the matter with you? What business have you with the Bible?" the Judge asks the plaintiff in the same hard and severe tone.

Since, with the courage of despair, she has been able to give utterance to her distress, her anxiety has decreased so that she can answer, "He must not take the oath!"

"Be silent, and put back the book!" demands the Judge.

She does not obey, but holds the book tightly with both hands. "He cannot take the oath!" she cries fiercely.

"Are you so determined to win your suit?" asks the Judge sharply.

"I want to withdraw the suit," she shrieks in

a high, shrill voice. "I don't want to force him to swear."

"What are you shrieking about?" demands the Judge. "Have you lost your senses?"

She catches her breath suddenly and tries to control herself. She hears herself how she is shrieking. The Judge will think she has gone mad if she cannot say what she would say calmly. She struggles with herself again to get control of her voice, and this time she succeeds. She says slowly, earnestly, and clearly, as she looks the Judge in the face: "I wish to withdraw the suit. He is the father of the child. I am still fond of him. I don't wish him to swear falsely."

She stands erect and resolute, facing the Judges' table, all the while looking the Judge square in the face. He sits with both hands resting on the table and for a long while does not take his eyes off from her. While the Judge is looking at her, a great change comes over him. All the ennui and displeasure in his face vanishes, and the large, rough-hewn visage becomes beautiful with the most beautiful emotion. "Ah, see!" he thinks — "Ah, see! such is the mettle of my people. I shall not be vexed at them when there is so much love and godliness even in one of the humblest."

Suddenly the Judge feels his eyes fill up with tears; then he pulls himself together, almost ashamed, and casts a hasty glance about him. He sees that the clerks and bailiffs and the whole long row of jurymen are leaning forward and looking at the girl who stands before the Judges' table with the Bible hugged close to her. And he sees a light in their faces, as though they had seen something very beautiful, which had made them happy all the way into their souls.

Then the Judge casts a glance over the spectators, and he sees that they all breathe a quick sigh of relief, as if they had just heard what they had longed above everything to hear.

Finally, the Judge looks at the defendant. Now it is *he* who stands with lowered head and looks at the floor.

The Judge turns once more to the poor girl. "It shall be as you wish," he says. "The case shall be stricken from the Calendar," — this to the recording clerk.

The defendant makes a move, as though he wished to interpose an objection. "Well, what now?" the Judge bellows at him. "Have you anything against it?"

The defendant's head hangs lower and lower, and he says, almost inaudibly, "Oh, no, I dare say it is best to let it go that way."

The Judge sits still a moment more, and then he pushes the heavy chair back, rises, and walks around the table and up to the plaintiff.

"Thank you!" he says and gives her his hand.

She has laid down the Bible and stands wiping away the tears with the crumpled up handkerchief.

"Thank you!" says the Judge once more, taking her hand and shaking it as if it belonged to a real man's man.

II

LET no one imagine that the girl who had passed through such a trying ordeal at the bar of justice thought that she had done anything praiseworthy! On the contrary, she considered herself disgraced before the whole court room. She did not understand that there was something honorable in the fact that the Judge had gone over and shaken hands with her. She thought it simply meant that the trial was over and that she might go her way.

Nor did she observe that people gave her kindly glances and that there were several who wanted to press her hand. She stole by and wanted only to go. There was a crush at the door. The court was over and many in their hurry to get out made a rush for the door. She drew aside and was about the last person to leave the court room because she felt that every one else ought to go before her.

When she finally came out, Gudmund Erlandsson's cart stood in waiting at the door. Gudmund was seated in the cart, holding the reins, and was apparently waiting for some one. As soon as he saw her among all the people who poured out of the court room, he called to her: "Come here, Helga! You can ride with me since we are going in the same direction."

Although she heard her name, she could not believe that it was she whom he was calling. It was not possible that Gudmund Erlandsson wanted to ride with her. He was the most attractive man in the whole parish, young and handsome and of good family connections and popular with every one. She could not imagine that he wished to associate with her.

She was walking with the head shawl drawn far down on her forehead, and was hastening past him without either glancing up or answering.

"Don't you hear, Helga, that you can ride with me?" said Gudmund, and there was a friendly note in his voice. But she could n't grasp that Gudmund meant well by her. She thought that, in one way or another, he wished to make sport of her and was only waiting for those who stood near by to begin tittering and laughing. She cast a frightened and indignant glance at him, and almost ran from the Court House grounds to be out of earshot when the laughter should start in.

Gudmund was unmarried at that time and lived at home with his parents. His father was a farm-owner. His was not a large farm and he was not rich, but he made a good living. The son had gone to the Court House to fetch some deeds for his father, but as there was also another purpose in the trip, he had groomed himself carefully. He had taken the brand-new trap with not a crack in the lacquering, had rubbed up the harness and curried the horse until he shone like satin. He had placed a bright red blanket on the seat beside him, and himself he had adorned with a short hunting-jacket, a small gray felt hat, and top boots, into which the trousers were tucked. This was no holiday attire, but he probably knew that he looked handsome and manly.

Gudmund was seated alone in the cart when he drove from home in the morning, but he had agreeable things to think of and the time had not seemed long to him. When he had arrived about half-way, he came across a poor young girl who was walking very slowly and looked as though she were scarcely able to move her feet because of exhaustion. It was autumn and the road was rain-soaked, and Gudmund saw how, with every step, she sank deeper into the mud. He stopped and asked where she was going. When he learned that she was on her way to the Court House, he invited her to ride. She thanked him and stepped up on the back of the cart to the narrow board where the hay sack was tied, as though she dared not touch the red blanket beside Gudmund. Nor was it his meaning that she should sit beside him. He did n't know who she was, but he supposed her to be the daughter of some poor backwoodsman and thought the rear of the cart was quite good enough for her.

When they came to a steep hill and the horse began to slow up, Gudmund started talking. He wanted to know her name and where she was from. When he learned that her name was Helga, and that she came from a backwoods farm called Big Marsh, he began to feel uneasy. "Have you always lived at home on the farm or have you been out to service?" he asked.

The past year she had been at home, but before this she had been working out.

"Where?" asked Gudmund hastily.

He thought it was a long while before the answer was forthcoming. "At the West Farm, with Per Mårtensson," she said finally, sinking her voice as if she would rather not have been heard.

But Gudmund heard her. "Indeed! Then it is you who —" said he, but did not conclude his meaning. He turned from her, and sat up straight in his seat and said not another word to her.

Gudmund gave the horse rap upon rap and talked loudly to himself about the wretched condition of the road and was in a very bad humor.

The girl sat still for a moment; presently Gudmund felt her hand upon his arm. "What do you wish?" he asked without turning his head.

Oh, he was to stop, so she could jump out.

"Why so?" sneered Gudmund. "Are n't you riding comfortably?"

"Yes, thank you, but I prefer to walk."

Gudmund struggled a little with himself. It was provoking that he should have bidden a person of Helga's sort to ride with him to-day of all days! But he thought also that since he had taken her into the wagon, he could not drive her out.

"Stop, Gudmund!" said the girl once again. She spoke in a very decided tone, and Gudmund drew in the reins.

"It is she, of course, who wishes to step down," thought he. "I don't have to force her to ride against her will."

She was down on the road before the horse had time to stop. "I thought you knew who I was when you asked me to ride," she said, "or I should not have stepped into the cart."

Gudmund muttered a short good-bye and drove on. She was doubtless right in thinking that he knew her. He had seen the girl from the marsh croft many times as a child, but she had changed since she was grown up. At first he was very glad to be rid of the travelling companion, but gradually he began to feel displeased with himself. He could hardly have acted differently, yet he did not like being cruel to any one.

Shortly after Gudmund had parted from Helga, he turned out of the road and up a narrow street, and came to a large and fine estate. As Gudmund drew up before the gate, the house door opened and one of the daughters appeared.

Gudmund raised his hat; at the same time a faint flush covered his face. ".Wonder if the Juryman is at home?" said he.

'No, father has gone down to the Court House," replied the daughter.

"Oh, then he has already gone," said Gudmund. "I drove over to ask if the Juryman would ride with me. I 'm going to the Court House."

"Father is always so punctual!" bewailed the daughter.

"It does n't matter," said Gudmund.

"Father would have been pleased, I dare say, to ride behind such a fine horse and in such a pretty cart as you have," remarked the girl pleasantly.

Gudmund smiled a little when he heard this commendation.

"Well, then, I must be off again," said he.

"Won't you step in, Gudmund?"

"Thank you, Hildur, but I 'm going to the Court House, you know. It won't do for me to be late."

Now Gudmund takes the direct road to the Court House. He was very well pleased with himself and thought no more of his meeting with Helga. It was fortunate that only Hildur had come out on the porch and that she had seen the

cart and blanket, the horse and harness. She
had probably taken note of everything.

This was the first time Gudmund had attended a Court. He thought that there was
much to see and learn, and remained the whole
day. He was sitting in the court room when
Helga's case came up; saw how she snatched
the Bible and hugged it close, and saw how she
defied both court attendants and Judge. When
it was all over and the Judge had shaken hands
with Helga, Gudmund rose quickly and went
out. He hurriedly hitched the horse to the
cart and drove up to the steps. He thought
Helga had been brave, and now he wished to
honor her. But she was so frightened that she
did not understand his purpose, and stole away
from his intended honor.

The same day Gudmund came to the marsh
croft late in the evening. It was a little croft,
which lay at the base of the forest ridge that
enclosed the parish. The road leading thither
was passable for a horse only in winter, and
Gudmund had to go there on foot. It was
difficult for him to find his way. He came near
breaking his legs on stumps and stones, and he
had to wade through brooks which crossed the
path in several places. Had it not been for the
bright moonlight, he could not have found his

way to the croft. He thought it was a very hard road that Helga had to tramp this day.

Big Marsh croft lay on the clearing about half-way up the ridge. Gudmund had never been there before, but he had often seen the place from the valley and was sufficiently familiar with it to know that he had gone aright.

All around the clearing lay a hedge of brushwood, which was very thick and difficult to get through. It was probably meant to be a kind of defence and protection against the whole wilderness that surrounded the croft. The cabin stood at the upper edge of the enclosure. Before it stretched a sloping house-yard covered with short, thick grass; and below the yard lay a couple of gray outhouses and a larder with a moss-covered roof. It was a poor and humble place, but one could n't deny that it was picturesque up there. The marsh, from which the croft had derived its name, lay somewhere near and sent forth mists which rose, beautiful, splendid, and silvery, in the moonlight, forming a halo around the marsh. The highest peak of the mountain loomed above the mist, and the ridge, prickly with pines, was sharply outlined against the horizon. Over the valley shone the moon. It was so light that one could distinguish fields and orchards and a winding brook, over

which the mists curled, like the faintest smoke.
It was not very far down there, but the peculiar
thing was that the valley lay like a world apart,
with which the forest and all that belonged to
it seemed to have nothing in common. It was
as if the people who lived here in the forest must
ever remain under the shadow of these trees.
They might find it quite as hard to feel contented down in the valley as woodcock and
eagle-owl and lynx and star-flowers.

Gudmund tramped across the open grass-plot
and up to the cabin. There a gleam of firelight
streamed through the window. As there were
no shades at the windows, he peeped into the
cabin to see if Helga was there. A small lamp
burned on the table near the window, and there
sat the master of the house, mending old shoes.
The mistress was seated farther back in the
room, close to the fireplace, where a slow fire
burned. The spinning-wheel was before her, but
she had paused in her work to play with a
little child. She had taken it up from the cradle,
and Gudmund heard how she prattled to it.
Her face was lined and wrinkled and she looked
severe. But, as she bent over the child, she had
a mild expression and she smiled as tenderly at
the little one as his own mother might have done.

Gudmund peered in, but could not see Helga

in any corner of the cabin. Then he thought it was best to remain outside until she came. He was surprised that she had not reached home. Perhaps she had stopped on the way somewhere to see an acquaintance and to get some food and rest? At all events, she would have to come back soon if she wished to be indoors before it was very late at night.

Gudmund stood still a moment and listened for footsteps. He thought that never before had he sensed such stillness. It was as though the whole forest held its breath and stood waiting for something extraordinary to happen.

No one tramped in the forest, no branch was broken, and no stone rolled down.

"Surely, Helga won't be long in coming! I wonder what she will say when she sees that I'm here?" thought Gudmund. "Perhaps she will scream and rush into the forest and will not dare come home the whole night!"

At the same time it struck him as rather strange that now, all of a sudden, he had so much business with that marsh croft girl!

On his return from the Court House to his home, he had, as usual, gone to his mother to relate his experiences of the day. Gudmund's mother was a sensible and broad-minded woman who had always understood how to treat her son, and he had as much confidence in her now as when he was a child. She had been an invalid for several years and could not walk, but sat all day in her chair. It was always a good hour for her when Gudmund came home from an outing and brought her the news.

When Gudmund had told his mother about Helga from Big Marsh, he observed that she became thoughtful. For a long while she sat quietly and looked straight ahead. "There seems to be something good in that girl still," she remarked. "It will never do to condemn a person because she has once met with misfortune. She might be very grateful to any one who helped her now."

Gudmund apprehended at once what his mother was thinking of. She could no longer help herself, but must have some one near her continually, and it was always difficult to find anybody who cared to remain in that capacity. His mother was exacting and not easy to get on with, and, moreover, all young folk preferred other work where they could have more freedom. Now, it must have occurred to his mother that she ought to take Helga from Big Marsh into her service, and Gudmund thought this a capital idea. Helga would certainly be very devoted to his mother.

"It will be hard for the child," remarked the mother after a little, and Gudmund understood that she was thinking seriously of the matter.

"Surely the parents would let it stay with them?" said Gudmund.

"It does not follow that she wants to part with it."

"She will have to give up thinking of what she wants or does n't want. I thought that she looked starved out. They can't have much to eat at the croft," said the son.

To this his mother made no reply, but began to talk of something else. It was evident that some new misgivings had come to her, which hindered her from coming to a decision.

Then Gudmund told her of how he had found a pretext for calling at the Juryman's at Älvåkra and had met Hildur. He mentioned what she had said of the horse and wagon, and it was easily seen that he was pleased with the meeting. His mother was also very much pleased. Where she sat in the cottage, unable to move from her chair, it was her constant occupation to spin plans for her son's future, and it was she who had first hit upon the idea that he should try and set his cap for the pretty daughter of the Juryman. It was the finest match he could make.

The Juryman was a yeoman farmer. He owned the largest farm in the parish and had much money and power. It was really absurd to hope that he would be satisfied with a son-in-law with no more wealth than Gudmund, but it was also possible that he would conform to his daughter's wishes. That Gudmund could win Hildur if he so wished, his mother was certain.

This was the first time Gudmund had betrayed to his mother that her thought had taken root in him, and they talked long of Hildur and of all the riches and advantages that would come to the chosen one. Soon there was another lull in the conversation, for his mother was again absorbed in her thoughts. "Could n't you send for this Helga? I should like to see her before taking her into my service," said the mother finally.

"It is well, mother, that you wish to take her under your wing," remarked Gudmund, thinking to himself that if his mother had a nurse with whom she was satisfied, his wife would have a pleasanter life here. "You 'll see that you will be pleased with the girl," he continued.

"Then, too, it would be a good deed to take her in hand," added the mother.

As it grew dusk, the invalid retired, and Gud-

mund went out to the stable to tend the horses.
It was beautiful weather, with a clear atmosphere, and the whole tract lay bathed in moonlight. It occurred to him that he ought to go
to Big Marsh to-night and convey his mother's
greeting. If the weather should continue clear
on the morrow, he would be so busy taking in
oats that neither he nor any one else would find
time to go there.

Now that Gudmund was standing outside the
cabin at Big Marsh croft listening, he certainly
heard no footsteps. But there were other
sounds which at short intervals pierced through
the stillness. He heard a soft weeping, a very
low and smothered moaning, with now and then
a sob. Gudmund thought that the sounds
came from the outhouse lane, and he walked
toward it. As he was nearing, the sobs ceased;
but it was evident that some one moved in the
woodshed. Gudmund seemed to comprehend
instantly who was there. "Is it you, Helga,
who sit here and weep?" asked Gudmund,
placing himself in the doorway so that the
girl could not rush away before he had spoken
with her.

Again it was perfectly still. Gudmund had
guessed rightly that it was Helga who sat there
and wept; but she tried to smother the sobs,

so that Gudmund would think he had heard wrongly and go away. It was pitch dark in the woodshed, and she knew that he could not see her.

But Helga was in such despair that evening it was not easy for her to keep back the sobs. She had not as yet gone into the cabin to see her parents. She had n't had the courage to go in. When she trudged up the steep hill in the twilight and thought of how she must tell her parents that she was not to receive any assistance from Per Mårtensson in the rearing of her child, she began to fear all the harsh and cruel things she felt they would say to her and thought of burying herself in the swamp. And in her terror she jumped up and tried to rush past Gudmund; but he was too alert for her. "Oh, no! You sha'n't get by before I have spoken with you."

"Only let me go!" she said, looking wildly at him.

"You look as though you wanted to jump into the river," said he; for now she was out in the moonlight and he could see her face.

"Well, what matters it if I did?" said Helga, throwing her head back and looking him straight in the eye. "This morning you did n't even care to have me ride on the back of your cart.

No one wants to have anything to do with me!
You must surely understand that it is best for
a miserable creature like me to put an end to
herself."

Gudmund did not know what to do next.
He wished himself far away, but he thought,
also, that he could not desert a person who was
in such distress. "Listen to me! Only promise that you will listen to what I have to
say to you; afterwards you may go wherever
you wish."

She promised.

"Is there anything here to sit on?"

"The chopping-block is over yonder."

"Then go over there and sit down and be
quiet!"

She went very obediently and seated herself.

"And don't cry any more!" said he, for he
thought he was beginning to get control over her.
But he should not have said this, for immediately
she buried her face in her hands and cried harder
than ever.

"Stop crying!" he said, ready to stamp his
foot at her. "There are those, I dare say, who
are worse off than you are."

"No, no one can be worse off!"

"You are young and strong. You should see
how my mother fares! She is so wasted from

suffering that she cannot move, but she never complains."

"She is not abandoned by everybody, as I am."

"You are not abandoned, either. I have spoken with my mother about you."

There was a pause in the sobs. One heard, as it were, the great stillness of the forest, which always held its breath and waited for something wonderful. "I was to say to you that you should come down to my mother to-morrow that she might see you. Mother thinks of asking if you would care to take service with us."

"Did she think of asking *me?*"

"Yes; but she wants to see you first."

"Does she know that — "

"She knows as much about you as all the rest do."

The girl leaped up with a cry of joy and wonderment, and the next moment Gudmund felt a pair of arms around his neck.* He was thoroughly frightened, and his first impulse was to break loose and run; but he calmed himself and stood still. He understood that the girl was so beside herself with joy that she did n't know what she was doing. At that moment she could have hugged the worst ruffian, only to find a little sympathy in the great happiness that had come to her.

"If she will take me into her service, I can live!" said she, burying her head on Gudmund's breast and weeping again. "You may know that I was in earnest when I wished to go down into the swamp," she said. "You deserve thanks for coming. You have saved my life." Until then Gudmund had been standing motionless, but now he felt that something tender and warm was beginning to stir within him. He raised his hand and stroked her hair. Then she started, as if awakened from a dream, and stood up straight as a rod before him. "You deserve thanks for coming," she repeated. She had become flame-red in the face, and he too reddened.

"Well, then, you will come home to-morrow," he said, putting out his hand to say good-bye.

"I shall never forget that you came to me to-night!" said Helga, and her great gratitude got the mastery over her shyness.

"Oh, yes, it was well perhaps that I came," he said quite calmly, and he felt rather pleased with himself. "You will go in now, of course?"

"Yes, now I shall go in."

Gudmund suddenly felt himself rather pleased with Helga too — as one usually is with a person whom one has succeeded in helping. She lingered and did not want to go. "I would like to see you safely under shelter before I leave."

"I thought they might retire before I went in."

"No, you must go in at once, so that you can have your supper and rest yourself," said he, thinking it was agreeable to take her in hand.

She went at once to the cabin, and he accompanied her, pleased and proud because she obeyed him.

When she stood on the threshold, they said good-bye to each other again; but before he had gone two paces, she came after him. "Remain just outside the door until I am in. It will be easier for me if I know that you are standing without."

"Yes," said he, "I shall stand here until you have come over the worst of it."

Then Helga opened the cabin door, and Gudmund noticed that she left it slightly ajar. It was as if she did not wish to feel herself separated from her helper who stood without. Nor did he feel any compunction about hearing all that happened within the cabin.

The old folks nodded pleasantly to Helga as she came in. Her mother promptly laid the child in the crib, and then went over to the cupboard and brought out a bowl of milk and a bread cake and placed them on the table.

"There! Now sit down and eat," said she. Then she went up to the fireplace and freshened

3

the fire. "I have kept the fire alive, so you could dry your feet and warm yourself when you came home. But eat something first! It is food that you need most."

All the while Helga had been standing at the door. "You must n't receive me so well, mother," she said in a low tone. "I will get no money from Per. I have renounced his help."

"There was some one here from the Court House this evening who had been there and heard how it turned out for you," said the mother. "We know all."

Helga was still standing by the door, looking out, as if she knew not which was in or out.

Then the farmer put down his work, pushed his spectacles up on his forehead, and cleared his throat for a speech of which he had been thinking the whole evening. "It is a fact, Helga," said he, "that mother and I have always wanted to be decent and honorable folk, but we have thought that we had been disgraced on your account. It was as though we had not taught you to distinguish between good and evil. But when we learned what you did to-day, we said to each other — mother and I — that now folks could see anyway that you have had a proper bringing up and right teaching, and we thought that perhaps we might yet be happy in you.

And mother did not want that we should go to bed before you came that you might have a hearty welcome home."

III

HELGA from the marsh croft came to När-lunda, and there all went well. She was willing and teachable and grateful for every kind word said to her. She always felt herself to be the humblest of mortals and never wanted to push herself ahead. It was not long until the household and the servants were satisfied with her.

The first days it appeared as if Gudmund was afraid to speak to Helga. He feared that this croft girl would get notions into her head because he had come to her assistance. But these were needless worries. Helga regarded him as altogether too fine and noble for her even to raise her eyes to. Gudmund soon perceived that he did not have to keep her at a distance. She was more shy of him than of any one else.

The autumn that Helga came to Närlunda, Gudmund paid many visits to Älvåkra, and there was much talk about the good chance he stood of being the prospective son-in-law of this estate. That the courtship had been successful all were assured at Christmas. Then the Juryman, with his wife and daughter, came over to Närlunda, and it was evident that they had come there to see how Hildur would fare if she married Gudmund.

This was the first time that Helga saw, at close range, her whom Gudmund was to marry. Hildur Ericsdotter was not yet twenty, but the marked thing about her was that no one could look at her without thinking what a handsome and dignified mistress she would be some day. She was tall and well built, fair and pretty, and apparently liked to have many about her to look after. She was never timid; she talked much and seemed to know everything better than the one with whom she was talking. She had attended school in the city for a couple of years and wore the prettiest frocks Helga had ever seen, but yet she did n't impress one as being showy or vain. Rich and beautiful as she was, she might have married a gentleman at any time, but she always declared that she did not wish to be a fine lady and sit with folded hands. She wanted to marry a farmer and look after her own house, like a real farmer's wife.

Helga thought Hildur a perfect wonder. Never had she seen any one who made such a superb appearance. Nor had she ever dreamed that a person could be so nearly perfect in every particular. To her it seemed a great joy that in the near future she was to serve such a mistress.

Everything had gone off well during the Juryman's visit. But whenever Helga looked back upon that day, she experienced a certain unrest. It seems that when the visitors had arrived, she had gone around and served coffee. When she came in with the tray, the Juryman's wife leaned forward and asked her mistress if she was not the girl from the marsh croft. She did not lower her voice much, and Helga had distinctly heard the question.

Mother Ingeborg answered yes, and then the other had said something which Helga could n't hear. But it was to the effect that she thought it singular they wanted a person of that sort in the house. This caused Helga many anxious moments. She tried to console herself with the thought that it was not Hildur, but her mother, who had said this.

One Sunday in the early spring Helga and Gudmund walked home together from church. As they came down the slope, they were with the other church people; but soon one after another dropped off until, finally, Helga and Gudmund were alone.

Then Gudmund happened to think that he

had not been alone with Helga since that night at
the croft, and the memory of that night came
forcibly back to him. He had thought of their
first meeting often enough during the winter, and
with it he had always felt something sweet and
pleasant thrill through his senses. As he went
about his work, he would call forth in thought
that whole beautiful evening: the white mist,
the bright moonlight, the dark forest heights,
the light valley, and the girl who had thrown
her arms round his neck and wept for joy. The
whole incident became more beautiful each time
that it recurred to his memory. But when Gudmund saw Helga going about among the others
at home, toiling and slaving, it was hard for him
to think that it was she who had shared in this.
Now that he was walking alone with her on the
church slope, he could n't help wishing for a
moment that she would be the same girl she
was on that evening.

Helga began immediately to speak of Hildur.
She praised her much: said she was the prettiest and most sensible girl in the whole parish,
and congratulated Gudmund because he would
have such an excellent wife. "You must tell her
to let me remain always at Närlunda," she said.
"It will be a pleasure to work for a mistress
like her."

Gudmund smiled at her enthusiasm, but answered only in monosyllables, as though he did not exactly follow her. It was well, of course, that she was so fond of Hildur, and so happy because he was going to be married.

"You have been content to be with us this winter?" he asked.

"Indeed I have! I cannot begin to tell you how kind mother Ingeborg and all of you have been to me!"

"Have you not been homesick for the forest?"

"Oh, yes, in the beginning, but not now any more."

"I thought that one who belonged to the forest could not help yearning for it."

Helga turned half round and looked at him, who walked on the other side of the road. Gudmund had become almost a stranger to her; but now there was something in his voice, his smile, that was familiar. Yes, he was the same man who had come to her and saved her in her greatest distress. Although he was to marry another, she was certain that he wanted to be a good friend to her, and a faithful helper.

She was very happy to feel that she could confide in him, as in none other, and thought that she must tell him of all that had happened to her since they last talked together. "I must tell you that it was rather hard for me the first weeks at Närlunda," she began. "But you must n't speak of this to your mother."

"If you want me to be silent, I'll be silent."

"Fancy! I was so homesick in the beginning that I was about to go back to the forest."

"Were you homesick? I thought you were glad to be with us."

"I simply could not help it," she said apologetically. "I understood, of course, how well it was for me to be here; you were all so good to me, and the work was not so hard but that I could manage with it, but I was homesick nevertheless. There was something that took hold of me and wanted to draw me back to the forest. I thought that I was deserting and betraying some one who had a right to me, when I wanted to stay here in the village."

"It was perhaps —" began Gudmund, but checked himself.

"No, it was not the boy I longed for. I knew that he was well cared for and that mother was kind to him. It was nothing in particular. I felt as though I were a wild bird that had been caged, and I thought I should die if I were not let out."

"To think that you had such a hard time of it!" said Gudmund smiling, for now, all at once, he recognized her. Now it was as if nothing had come between them, but that they had parted at the forest farm the evening before.

Helga smiled again, but continued to speak of her torments. "I did n't sleep a single night," said she, "and as soon as I went to bed, the tears started to flow, and when I got up of a morning, the pillow was wet through. In the daytime, when I went about among all of you, I could keep back the tears, but as soon as I was alone my eyes would fill up."

"You have wept much in your time," said Gudmund without looking the least bit sympathetic as he pronounced the words.

Helga thought that he was laughing to himself all the while. "You surely don't comprehend how hard it was for me!" she said, speaking faster and faster in her effort to make him understand her. "A great longing took possession of me and carried me out of myself. Not for a moment could I feel happy! Nothing was beautiful, nothing was a pleasure; not a human being could I become attached to. You all remained just as strange to me as you were the first time I entered the house."

"But did n't you say a moment ago that you

wished to remain with us?" said Gudmund wonderingly.

"Of course I did!"

"Then, surely, you are not homesick now?"

"No, it has passed over. I have been cured. Wait, and you shall hear!"

As she said this, Gudmund crossed to the other side of the road and walked beside her, laughing to himself all the while. He seemed glad to hear her speak, but probably he did n't attach much importance to what she was relating. Gradually Helga took on his mood, and she thought everything was becoming easy and light. The church road was long and difficult to walk, but to-day she was not tired. There was something that carried her. She continued with her story because she had begun it, but it was no longer of much importance to her to speak. It would have been quite as agreeable to her if she might have walked silently beside him.

"When I was the most unhappy," she said, "I asked mother Ingeborg one Saturday evening to let me go home and remain over Sunday. And that evening, as I tramped over the hills to the marsh, I believed positively that I should never again go back to Närlunda. But at home father and mother were so happy because I

had found service with good and respectable
people, that I did n't dare tell them I could not
endure remaining with you. Then, too, as soon
as I came up into the forest all the anguish and
pain vanished entirely. I thought the whole
thing had been only a fancy. And then it was
so difficult about the child. Mother had become
attached to the boy and had made him her own.
He was n't mine any more. And it was well
thus, but it was hard to get used to."

"Perhaps you began to be homesick for us?"
blurted Gudmund.

"Oh, no! On Monday morning, as I awoke
and thought of having to return to you, the
longing came over me again. I lay crying and
fretting because the only right and proper thing
for me to do was to go back to Närlunda. But
I felt all the same as though I were going to be
ill or lose my senses if I went back. Suddenly
I remembered having once heard some one say
that if one took some ashes from the hearth
in one's own home and strewed them on the
fire in the strange place, one would be rid of
homesickness."

"Then it was a remedy that was easy to take,"
said Gudmund.

"Yes, but it was supposed to have this effect
also: afterwards one could never be content in

any other place. If one were to move from the homestead to which one had borne the ashes, one must long to get back there again just as much as one had longed before to get away from there."

"Could n't one carry ashes along wherever one moved to?"

"No, it can't be done more than once. Afterwards there is no turning back, so it was a great risk to try anything like that."·

"I should n't have taken chances on a thing of that kind," said Gudmund, and she could hear that he was laughing at her.

"But I dared, all the same," retorted Helga. "It was better than having to appear as an ingrate in your mother's eyes and in yours, when you had tried to help me. I brought a little ashes from home, and when I got back to Närlunda I watched my opportunity, when no one was in, and scattered the ashes over the hearth."

"And now you believe it is ashes that have helped you?"

"Wait, and you shall hear how it turned out! Immediately I became absorbed in my work and thought no more about the ashes all that day. I grieved exactly as before and was just as weary of everything as I had been. There was much to be done that day, both in the house and out of it, and when I finished with the evening's milking and was going in, the fire on the hearth was already lighted."

"Now I'm very curious to hear what happened," said Gudmund.

"Think! Already, as I was crossing the house yard, I thought there was something familiar in the gleam from the fire, and when I opened the door, it flashed across my mind that I was going into our own cabin and that father and mother would be sitting by the hearth. This flew past like a dream, but when I came in, I was surprised that it looked so pretty and homelike in the cottage. To me your mother and the rest of you had never appeared as pleasant as you did in the firelight. It seemed really good to come in, and this was not so before. I was so astonished that I could hardly keep from clapping my hands and shouting. I thought you were all so changed. You were no longer strangers to me and I could talk to you about all sorts of things. You can understand, of course, that I was happy, but I could n't help being astonished. I wondered if I had been bewitched, and then I remembered the ashes I had strewn over the hearth."

"Yes, it was marvellous," said Gudmund.

He did not believe the least little bit in witch-craft and was not at all superstitious; but he did n't dislike hearing Helga talk of such things. "Now the wild forest girl has returned," thought he. "Can anybody comprehend how one who has passed through all that she has can still be so childish?"

"Of course it was wonderful!" said Helga. "And the same thing has been coming back all winter. As soon as the fire on the hearth was burning, I felt the same confidence and security as if I had been at home. But there must be something extraordinary about this fire — not with any other kind of fire, perhaps — only that which burns on a hearth, with all the house-hold gathered around it, night after night. It gets sort of acquainted with one. It plays and dances for one and talks to one, and sometimes it is ill-humored. It is as if it had the power to create comfort and discomfort. I thought now that the fire from home had come to me and that it gave the same glow of pleasure to every one here that it had done back home."

"What if you had to leave Närlunda?" said Gudmund.

"Then I must long to come back again all my life," said she. And the quiver in her voice betrayed that this was spoken in profound seriousness.

"Well, I shall not be the one to drive you away!" said Gudmund. Although he was laughing, there was something warm in his tone.

They started no new subject of conversation, but walked on in silence until they came to the homestead. Now and then Gudmund turned his head to look at her who was walking at his side. She had gathered strength after her hard time of the year before. Her features were delicate and refined; her hair was like an aureole around her head, and her eyes were not easy to read. Her step was light and elastic, and when she spoke, the words came readily, yet modestly. She was afraid of being laughed at, still she had to speak out what was in her heart.

Gudmund wondered if he wished Hildur to be like this, but he probably did n't. This Helga would be nothing special to marry.

A fortnight later Helga heard that she must leave Närlunda in April because Hildur Erics-dotter would not live under the same roof with her. The master and mistress of the house did not say this in so many words, but the mistress hinted that when the new daughter-in-law came, they would in all probability get so much help from her they would not require so many ser-vants. On another occasion she said she had heard of a good place where Helga would fare better than with them.

It was not necessary for Helga to hear anything further to understand that she must leave, and she immediately announced that she would move, but she did not wish any other situation and would return to her home.

It was apparent that it was not of their own free will they were dismissing Helga from Närlunda.

When she was leaving, there was a spread for her. It was like a party, and mother Ingeborg gave her such heaps of dresses and shoes that she, who had come to them with only a bundle under her arm, could now barely find room enough in a chest for her possessions.

"I shall never again have such an excellent servant in my house as you have been," said mother Ingeborg. "And do not think too hard of me for letting you go! You understand, no doubt, that it is not my will, this. I shall not forget you. So long as I have any power, you shall never have to suffer want."

She arranged with Helga that she was to weave sheets and towels for her. She gave her employment for at least half a year.

Gudmund was in the woodshed splitting wood the day Helga was leaving. He did not come

in to say good-bye, although his horse was at
the door. He appeared to be so busy that he
did n't take note of what was going on. She
had to go out to him to say farewell.

He laid down the axe, took Helga's hand, and
said rather hurriedly, "Thank you for all!" and
began chopping again. Helga had wanted to
say something about her understanding that it
was impossible for them to keep her and that
it was all her own fault. She had brought this
upon herself. But Gudmund chopped away
until the splinters flew around him, and she
could n't make up her mind to speak.

But the strangest thing about this whole
moving affair was that the master himself, old
Erland Erlandsson, drove Helga up to the
marsh.

Gudmund's father was a little weazened man,
with a bald pate and beautiful and knowing
eyes. He was very timid, and so reticent at
times that he did not speak a word the whole
day. So long as everything went smoothly,
one took no notice of him, but when anything
went wrong, he always said and did what there
was to be said and done to right matters. He
was a capable accountant and enjoyed the confidence of every man in the township. He exe-
cuted all kinds of public commissions and was

4

more respected than many a man with a large estate and great riches.

Erland Erlandsson drove Helga home in his own wagon, and he would n't allow her to step down and walk up any of the hills. When they arrived at the marsh croft, he sat a long while in the cabin and talked with Helga's parents, telling them of how pleased he and mother Ingeborg had been with her. It was only because they did not need so many servants that they were sending her home. She, who was the youngest, must go. They had felt that it was wrong to dismiss any of those who were old in their service.

Erland Erlandsson's speech had the desired effect, and the parents gave Helga a warm welcome. When they heard that she had received such large orders that she could support herself with weaving, they were satisfied, and she remained at home.

IV

GUDMUND thought that he had loved Hildur until the day when she exacted from him the promise that Helga should be sent away from Närlunda ; at least up to that time there was no one whom he had esteemed more highly

than Hildur. No other young girl, to his thinking, could come up to her. It had been a pleasure
for him to picture a future with Hildur. They
would be rich and looked up to, and he felt
instinctively that the home Hildur managed
would be good to live in. He liked also to
think that he would be well supplied with money
after he had married her. He could then improve
the land, rebuild all the tumble-down houses,
extend the farm, and be a real landed proprietor.

The same Sunday that he had walked home
from church with Helga, he had driven over
to Älvåkra in the evening. Then Hildur had
started talking about Helga and had said that
she would n't come to Närlunda until that girl
was sent away. At first Gudmund had tried
to dismiss the whole matter as a jest, but it
was soon obvious that Hildur was in earnest.
Gudmund pleaded Helga's cause exceedingly
well and remarked that she was very young
when first sent out to service and it was not
strange that things went badly when she came
across such a worthless fellow as Per Mårtensson.
But since his mother had taken her in hand,
she had always conducted herself well. " It
can't be right to push her out," said he. " Then,
perhaps, she might meet with misfortune again."

But Hildur would not yield. " If that girl

is to remain at Närlunda, then I will never come there," she declared. "I cannot tolerate a person of that kind in my home."

"You don't know what you are doing," said Gudmund. "No one understands so well as Helga how to care for mother. We have all been glad that she came to us. Before she came, mother was often peevish and depressed."

"I shall not compel you to send her away," said Hildur, but it was clear that if Gudmund were to take her at her word, in this instance, she was ready to break the engagement.

"It will probably have to be as you wish," said Gudmund. He did not feel that he could jeopardize his whole future for Helga's sake, but he was very pale when he acquiesced, and he was silent and low-spirited the entire evening.

It was this which had caused Gudmund to fear that perhaps Hildur was not altogether what he had fancied her. He did not like, I dare say, that she had pitted her will against his. But the worst of it was that he could not comprehend anything else than that she was in the wrong. He felt that he would willingly have given in to her had she been broad-minded, but instead, it seemed to him, she was only petty and heartless. Once his doubts were awakened, it was not long before he perceived one thing

and another which were not as he wished.
"Doubtless she is one of those who think first
and foremost of themselves," he muttered
every time he parted from her, and he wondered
how long her love for him would last if it were
put to the test. He tried to console himself
with the idea that all people thought of themselves first, but instantly Helga flashed into his
mind. He saw her as she stood in the court
room and snatched the Bible, and heard how
she cried out: " I withdraw the suit. I am still
fond of him and I don't want him to swear
falsely." It was thus he would have Hildur.
Helga had become for him a standard by which
he measured people. Though certainly there
were many who were equal to her in affection!

Day by day he thought less of Hildur, but it
did not occur to him that he should relinquish
his prospective bride. He tried to imagine his
discouragement was simply an idle whim. Only
a few weeks ago he regarded her as the best in
the world!

Had this been at the beginning of the courtship, he would have withdrawn, perhaps, but
now the banns were already published and the
wedding day fixed, and in his home they had
begun repairing and rebuilding. Nor did he
wish to forfeit the wealth and the good social

position which awaited him. What excuse could he offer for breaking the engagement? That which he had to bring against Hildur was so inconsequential that it would have turned to air on his lips had he attempted to express it.

But the heart of him was often heavy, and every time he had an errand down to the parish or the city he bought ale or wine at the shops to drink himself into a good humor. When he had emptied a couple of bottles, he was again proud of the marriage and pleased with Hildur. Then he did n't understand what it was that pained him.

Gudmund often thought of Helga and longed to meet her. But he fancied that Helga believed him a wretch because he had not kept the promise which he voluntarily made her, but had allowed her to go away. He could neither explain nor excuse himself, therefore he avoided her.

One morning, when Gudmund was walking up the road, he met Helga, who had been down in the village to buy milk. Gudmund turned about and joined her.

She did n't appear to be pleased with his company and walked rapidly, as if she wished to get away from him, and said nothing. Gudmund, too, kept still because he did n't quite know how he should begin the conversation.

A vehicle was seen on the road, far behind. Gudmund was absorbed in thought and did not mark it, but Helga had seen it and turned abruptly to him: "It is not worth your while to be in my company, Gudmund, for, unless I see wrongly, it is the Juryman from Älvåkra and his daughter who come driving back there."

Gudmund glanced up quickly, recognized the horse, and made a movement as if to turn back; but the next instant he straightened up and walked calmly at Helga's side until the vehicle had passed. Then he slackened his pace. Helga continued to walk rapidly, and they parted company without his having said a word to her. But all that day he was better satisfied with himself than he had been in a long while.

V

IT was decided that Gudmund and Hildur's wedding should be celebrated at Älvåkra the day following Palm Sunday. On the Friday before, Gudmund drove to town to make some purchases for the home-coming banquet, which was to be held at Närlunda the day after the wedding. In the village he happened across a number of young men from his parish. They knew it was his last trip to the city before the marriage and made it the occasion for a carouse. All insisted that Gudmund must drink, and they succeeded finally in getting him thoroughly intoxicated.

He came home on Saturday morning so late that his father and the men servants had already gone out to their work, and he slept on until late in the afternoon. When he arose and was going to dress himself, he noticed that his coat was torn in several places. "It looks as though I had been in a fight last night," said he, trying to recall what he had been up to. He remembered this much: he had left the public tavern at eleven o'clock in company with his comrades; but where they had gone afterwards, he could n't remember. It was like trying to peer into a great darkness. He did not know if they had only driven around on the streets or if they had been in somebody's home. He did n't remember whether he or some one else had harnessed the horse and had no recollection whatever of the drive home.

When he came into the living-room of the cottage, it was scoured and arranged for the occasion. All work was over for the day, and the household were having coffee. No one spoke of Gudmund's trip. It seemed to be a matter agreed upon that he should have the freedom of living as he chose these last weeks.

Gudmund sat down at the table and had his coffee like the others. As he sat pouring it from the cup into the saucer and back into the cup again to let it cool, mother Ingeborg, who had finished with hers, took up the newspaper, which had just arrived, and began reading. She read aloud column after column, and Gudmund, his father, and the rest sat and listened.

Among other things which she read, there was an account of a fight that had taken place the night before, on the big square, between a gang of drunken farmers and some laborers. As soon as the police turned up, the fighters fled, but one of them lay dead on the square. The man was carried to the police station, and when no outward injury was found on him, they had tried to resuscitate him. But all attempts had been in vain, and at last they discovered that a knife-blade was imbedded in the skull. It was the blade of an uncommonly large clasp-knife that had pierced the brain and was broken off close to the head. The murderer had fled with the knife-handle, but as the police knew perfectly well who had been in the fight, they had hopes of soon finding him.

While mother Ingeborg was reading this,

Gudmund set down the coffee-cup, stuck his hand in his pocket, pulled out a clasp-knife, and glanced at it carelessly. But almost immediately he started, turned the knife over, and poked it into his pocket as quickly as though it had burned him. He did not touch the coffee after that, but sat a long while, perfectly still, with a puzzled expression on his face. His brows were contracted, and it was apparent that he was trying with all his might to think out something.

Finally he stood up, stretched himself, yawned, and walked leisurely toward the door. "I 'll have to bestir myself. I have n't been out of doors all day," he said, leaving the room.

About the same time Erland Erlandsson also arose. He had smoked out his pipe, and now he went into the side room to get some tobacco. As he was standing in there, refilling his pipe, he saw Gudmund walking along. The windows of the side room did not, like those of the main room, face the yard, but looked out upon a little garden plot with a couple of tall apple trees. Beyond the plot lay a bit of swamp land where in the spring of the year there were big pools of water, but which were almost dried out in the summer. Toward this side it was seldom that any one went. Erland Erlandsson wondered what Gudmund was doing there, and followed him with his eyes. Then he saw that the son stuck his hand into his pocket, drew out some object, and flung it away in the morass. Thereupon he walked back across the little garden plot, leaped a fence, and went down the road.

As soon as his son was out of sight, Erland, in his turn, betook himself, as he should have done, to the swamp. He waded out into the mire, bent down, and picked up something his foot had touched. It was a large clasp-knife with the biggest blade broken off. He turned it over and over and examined it carefully while he still stood in the water. Then he put it into his pocket, but he took it out again and looked at it before returning to the house.

Gudmund did not come home until the household had retired. He went immediately to bed without touching his supper, which was spread in the main room.

Erland Erlandsson and his wife slept in the side room. At daybreak Erland thought he heard footsteps outside the window. He got up, drew aside the curtain, and saw Gudmund walking down to the swamp. He stripped off stockings and shoes and waded out into the water, tramping back and forth, like one who is searching for something. He kept this up for a long

while, then he walked back to dry land, as if he
intended to go away, but soon turned back to
resume his search. A whole hour his father
stood watching him. Then Gudmund went
back to the house again and to bed.

On Palm Sunday Gudmund was to drive to
church. As he started to hitch up the horse, his
father came out. "You have forgotten to polish
the harness to-day," he said, as he walked by;
for both harness and cart were muddy.

"I have had other things to think of," said
Gudmund listlessly, and drove off without
doing anything in the matter.

After the service Gudmund accompanied his
betrothed to Älvåkra and remained there all
day. A number of young people came to celebrate Hildur's last evening as a maid, and there
was dancing till far into the night. Intoxicants
were plentiful, but Gudmund did not touch
them. The whole evening he had scarcely
spoken a word to any one, but he danced wildly
and laughed at times, loudly and stridently,
without any one's knowing what he was so
amused over.

Gudmund did not come home until about
two in the morning, and when he had stabled
the horse he went down to the swamp back of
the house. He took off his shoes and stockings,

rolled up his trousers, and waded into the water and mud. It was a light spring night, and his father was standing in the side room behind the curtain, watching his son. He saw how he walked bending over the water and searching as on the previous night. He went up on land between times, but after a moment or two he would wade again through the mud. Once he went and fetched a bucket from the barn and began dipping water from the pools, as if he intended to drain them, but really found it unprofitable and set the bucket aside. He tried also with a pole-net. He ploughed through the entire swamp-ground with it, but seemed to bring up nothing but mud. He did not go in until the morning was so well on that the people in the house were beginning to bestir themselves. Then he was so tired and spent that he staggered as he walked, and he flung himself upon the bed without undressing

When the clock struck eight, his father came and waked him. Gudmund lay upon the bed, his clothing covered with mud and clay, but his father did not ask what he had been doing. He simply said, "It is time now to get up," and closed the door.

After a while Gudmund came down stairs, dressed in his wedding clothes. He was pale, and his eyes wore a troubled expression, but no one had ever seen him look so handsome. His features were as if illumined by an inner light. One felt that one was looking upon something no longer made up of flesh and blood, — only of soul and will.

It was solemnly ceremonious down in the main room. His mother was in black, and she had thrown a pretty silk shawl across her shoulders, although she was not to be at the wedding. Fresh birch leaves were arranged in the fireplace. The table was spread, and there was a great quantity of food.

When they had breakfasted, mother Ingeborg read a hymn and something from the Bible. Then she turned to Gudmund, thanked him for having been a good son, wished him happiness in his new life, and gave him her blessing. Mother Ingeborg could arrange her words well, and Gudmund was deeply moved. The tears welled to his eyes time and again, but he managed to choke them back. His father, too, said a few words. "It will be hard for your parents to lose you," he said, and again Gudmund came near breaking down. All the servants came forward and shook hands with him and thanked him for the past. Tears were in his eyes all the while. He pulled himself together and made several attempts to speak, but could scarcely get a word past his lips.

His father was to accompany him to the wedding and be one of the party. He went out and harnessed the horse, after which he came back and announced that it was time to start. When Gudmund was seated in the cart, he noticed that it was cleansed and burnished. Everything was as bright and shiny as he himself always wished it to be. At the same time he saw, also, how neat everything about the place looked. The driveway had been laid with new gravel; piles of old wood and rubbish, which had lain there all his life, were removed. On each side of the entrance door stood a birch branch, as a gate of honor. A large wreath of blueberry hung on the weather-vane, and from every aperture peeped light green birch-leaves. Again Gudmund was ready to burst into tears. He grasped his father's hand hard when he was about to start; it was as though he wished to prevent his going.

"Is there something —?" said the father.

"Oh, no!" said Gudmund. "It is best, I dare say, that we go ahead."

Gudmund had to say one more farewell before he was very far from the homestead. It was Helga from Big Marsh, who stood waiting at the hedge, where the foliage path leading from her home opened into the highway. The father was driving and stopped when he saw Helga.

"I have been waiting for you, as I wanted to wish you happiness to-day," said Helga.

Gudmund leaned far out over the cart and shook hands with Helga. He thought that she had grown thin and that her eyelids were red. Very probably she had lain awake and cried all night and was homesick for Närlunda. But now she tried to appear happy and smiled sweetly at him. Again he felt deeply moved but could not speak.

His father, who was reputed never to speak a word until it was called forth by extreme necessity, joined in: "That good wish, I think, Gudmund will be more glad over than any other."

"Yes, of that you may be sure!" said Gudmund. He shook hands with Helga once more, and then they drove on.

Gudmund leaned back in the cart and looked after Helga. When she was hidden from view by a couple of trees, he hastily tore aside the apron of the carriage, as if he wished to jump out.

"Is there anything more you wish to say to Helga?" asked his father.

"No, oh, no!" answered Gudmund and turned round again.

Suddenly Gudmund leaned his head against his father's shoulder and burst out crying.

"What ails you?" asked Erland Erlandsson, drawing in the reins so suddenly that the horse stopped.

"Oh, they are all so good to me and I don't deserve it."

"But you have never done anything wrong, surely?"

"Yes, father, I have."

"That we can't believe."

"I have killed a human being!"

The father drew a deep breath. It sounded almost like a sigh of relief, and Gudmund raised his head, astonished, and looked at him. His father set the horse in motion again; then he said calmly, "I 'm glad you have told of this yourself."

"Did you know it already, father?"

"I surmised last Saturday evening that there was something wrong. And then I found your knife down in the morass."

"So it was you who found the knife!"

"I found it and I noticed that one of the blades had been broken off."

"Yes, father, I 'm aware that the knife-blade

5

is gone, but still I cannot get it into my head that
I did it."

"It was probably done in the drunkenness and
delirium."

"I know nothing; I remember nothing. I
could see by my clothes that I had been in a
fight and I knew that the knife-blade was
missing."

"I understand that it was your intention to
be silent about this," said the father.

"I thought that perhaps the rest of the party
were as irresponsible as myself and *I* could n't
remember anything. There was perhaps no
other evidence against me than the knife, therefore I threw it away."

"I comprehend that you must have reasoned
in that way."

"You understand, father, that I do not know
who is dead. I had never seen him before, I
dare say. I have no recollection of having done
it. I did n't think I ought to suffer for what I
had not done knowingly. But soon I got to
thinking that I must have been mad to throw
the knife into the marsh. It dries out in summer, and then any one might find it. I tried last
night and the night before to find it."

"Did n't it occur to you that you should
confess?"

"No! Yesterday I thought only of how I could keep it a secret, and I tried to dance and be merry, so that no one would mark any change in me."

"Was it your intention to go to the bridal altar to-day without confessing? You were assuming a grave responsibility. Did n't you understand that if you were discovered you would drag Hildur and her kin with you into misery?"

"I thought that I was sparing them most by saying nothing."

They drove now as fast as possible. The father seemed to be in haste to arrive, and all the time he talked with his son. He had not said so much to him in all his life before.

"I wonder how you came to think differently?" said he.

"It was because Helga came and wished me luck. Then there was something hard in me that broke. I was touched by something in her. Mother, also, moved me this morning, and I wanted to speak out and tell her that I was not worthy of your love; but then the hardness was still within me and made resistance. But when Helga appeared, it was all over with me. I felt that she really ought to be angry with me who was to blame for her having to leave our home."

"Now I think you are agreed with me that we

must let the Juryman know this at once," said
the father.

"Yes," answered Gudmund in a low tone.
"Why, certainly!" he added almost immediately after, louder and firmer. "I don't want
to drag Hildur into my misfortune. This she
would never forgive me."

"The Älvåkra folk are jealous of their honor,
like the rest," remarked the father. "And you
may as well know, Gudmund, that when I left
home this morning I was thinking that I must
tell the Juryman your position if you did not decide to do so yourself. I never could have stood
silently by and let Hildur marry a man who at
any moment might be accused of murder."

He cracked the whip and drove on, faster and
faster. "This will be the hardest thing for you,"
said he, "but we'll try and have it over with
quickly. I believe that, to the Juryman's mind,
it will be right for you to give yourself up, and
they will be kind to you, no doubt."

Gudmund said nothing. His torture increased
the nearer they approached Älvåkra. The
father continued talking to keep up his courage.

"I have heard something of this sort before,"
said he. "There was a bridegroom once who
happened to shoot a comrade to death during a
hunt. He did not do it intentionally, and it was

not discovered that he was the one who had fired the fatal shot. But a day or two later he was to be married, and when he came to the home of the bride, he went to her and said: 'The marriage cannot take place. I do not care to drag you into the misery which awaits me.' But she stood, dressed in bridal wreath and crown, and took him by the hand and led him into the drawing-room, where the guests were assembled and all was in readiness for the ceremony. She related in a clear voice what the bridegroom had just said to her. 'I have told of this, that all may know you have practised no deceit on me.' Then she turned to the bridegroom. 'Now I want to be married to you at once. You are what you are, even though you have met with misfortune, and whatever awaits you, I want to share it equally with you.'"

Just as the father had finished the narrative, they were on the long avenue leading to Älvåkra. Gudmund turned to him with a melancholy smile. "It will not end thus for us," he said.

"Who knows?" said the father, straightening in the cart. He looked upon his son and was again astonished at his beauty this day. "It would not surprise me if something great and unexpected were to come to him," thought he.

There was to have been a church ceremony,

and already a crowd of people were gathered at the bride's home to join in the wedding procession. A number of the Juryman's relatives from a distance had also arrived. They were sitting on the porch in their best attire, ready for the drive to church. Carts and carriages were strung out in the yard, and one could hear the horses stamping in the stable as they were being curried. The parish fiddler sat on the steps of the storehouse alone, tuning his fiddle. At a window in the upper story of the cottage stood the bride, dressed and waiting to have a peep at the bridegroom before he had time to discover her.

Erland and Gudmund stepped from the carriage and asked immediately for a private conference with Hildur and her parents. Soon they were all standing in the little room which the Juryman used as his study.

"I think you must have read in the papers of that fight in town last Saturday night, where a man was killed," said Gudmund, as rapidly as if he were repeating a lesson.

"Oh, yes, I 've read about it, of course," said the Juryman.

"I happened to be in town that night," continued Gudmund. Now there was no response. It was as still as death. Gudmund thought they all glared at him with such fury that he was unable to continue. But his father came to his aid.

"Gudmund had been invited out by a few friends. He had probably drunk too much that night, and when he came home he did not know what he had been doing. But it was apparent that he had been in a fight, for his clothes were torn."

Gudmund saw that the dread which the others felt increased with every word that was said, but he himself was growing calmer. There awoke in him a sense of defiance, and he took up the words again: "When the paper came on Saturday evening and I read of the fight and of the knife-blade which was imbedded in the man's skull, I took out my knife and saw that a blade was missing."

"It is bad news that Gudmund brings with him," said the Juryman. "It would have been better had he told us of this yesterday."

Gudmund was silent; and now his father came to the rescue again. "It was not so easy for Gudmund. It was a great temptation to keep quiet about the whole affair. He is losing much by this confession."

"We may be glad that he has spoken now, and that we have not been tricked and dragged into this wretched affair," said the Juryman bitterly.

Gudmund kept his eyes fixed on Hildur all the while. She was adorned with veil and crown, and now he saw how she raised her hand and drew out one of the large pins which held the crown in place. She seemed to do this unconsciously. When she observed that Gudmund's glance rested upon her, she stuck the pin in again.

"It is not yet fully proved that Gudmund is the slayer," said his father, "but I can well understand that you wish the wedding postponed until everything has been cleared up."

"It is not worth while to talk of postponement," said the Juryman. "I think that Gudmund's case is clear enough for us to decide that all is over between him and Hildur now."

Gudmund did not at once reply to this judgment. He walked over to his betrothed and put out his hand. She sat perfectly still and seemed not to see him. "Won't you say farewell to me, Hildur?"

Then she looked up, and her large eyes stared coldly at him. "Was it with that hand you guided the knife?" she asked.

Gudmund did not answer her, but turned to the Juryman. "Now I am sure of my case," he said. "It is useless to talk of a wedding."

With this the conference was ended, and Gudmund and Erland went their way.

They had to pass through a number of rooms and corridors before they came out, and everywhere they saw preparations for the wedding. The door leading to the kitchen was open, and they saw many bustling about in eager haste. The smell of roasts and of baking penetrated the air; the whole fireplace was covered with large and small pots and pans, and the copper saucepans, which usually decorated the walls, were down and in use. "Fancy, it is for my wedding that they are puttering like this!" thought Gudmund, as he was passing.

He caught a glimpse, so to speak, of all the wealth of this old peasant estate as he wandered through the house. He saw the dining-hall, where the long tables were set with a long row of silver goblets and decanters. He passed by the clothes-press, where the floor was covered with great chests and where the walls were hung with an endless array of wearing apparel. When he came out in the yard, he saw many vehicles, old and new, and fine horses being led out from the stable, and gorgeous carriage robes placed in the carriages. He looked out across a couple of farms with cow-sheds, barns, sheep-folds, storehouses, sheds, larders, and many other buildings. "All this might have been mine," he thought, as he seated himself in the cart.

Suddenly he was seized with a sense of bitter regret. He would have liked to throw himself out of the cart and go in and say that what he had told them was not true. He had only wished to joke with them and frighten them. It was awfully stupid of him to confess. Of what use had it been to him to confess? The dead was dead. No, this confession carried nothing with it save his ruin.

These last weeks he had not been very enthusiastic over this marriage. But now, when he must renounce it, he realized what it was worth to him. It meant much to lose Hildur Ericsdotter and all that went with her. What did it matter that she was domineering and opinionated? She was still the peer of all in these regions, and through her he would have come by great power and honor.

It was not only Hildur and her possessions he was missing, but minor things as well. At this moment he should have been driving to the church, and all who looked upon him would have envied him. And it was to-day that he should have sat at the head of the wedding table and been in the thick of the dancing and the gayety. It was his great luck-day that was going from him.

Erland turned time and again to his son and looked at him. Now he was not so handsome or transfigured as he had been in the morning, but sat there listless and heavy and dull-eyed. The father wondered if the son regretted having confessed and meant to question him about it, but thought it best to be silent.

"Where are we driving to now?" asked Gudmund presently. "Would n't it be as well to go at once to the sheriff?"

"You had better go home first and have a good sleep," said the father. "You have not had much sleep these last nights, I dare say."

"Mother will be frightened when she sees us."

"She won't be surprised," answered the father, "for she knows quite as much as I do. She will be glad, of course, that you have confessed."

"I believe mother and the rest of you at home are glad to get me into prison," snarled Gudmund.

"We know that you are losing a good deal in acting rightly," said the father. "We can't help but be glad because you have conquered yourself."

Gudmund felt that he could not endure going home and having to listen to all who would commend him because he had spoiled his future.

He sought some excuse that he might escape meeting any one until he had recovered his poise. Then they drove by the place where the path led to Big Marsh. "Will you stop here, father? I think I'll run up to see Helga and have a talk with her."

Willingly the father reined in the horse. "Only come home as quickly as you can, that you may rest yourself," said he.

Gudmund went into the woods and was soon out of sight. He did not think of seeking Helga; he was only thinking of being alone, so that he would n't have to control himself. He felt an unreasonable anger toward everything, kicked at stones that lay in his path, and paused sometimes to break off a big branch only because a leaf had brushed his cheek.

He followed the path to Big Marsh, but walked past the croft and up the hill which lay above it. He had wandered off the path, and in order to reach the hill-top he must cross a broad ridge of sharp, jagged rocks. It was a hazardous tramp over the sharp rock edges. He might have broken both arms and legs had he made a misstep. He understood this perfectly, but went on as if it amused him to run into danger. "If I were to fall and hurt myself, no one can find me up here," thought he. "What of it? I may as well die here as to sit for years within prison walls."

All went well, however, and a few moments later he was up on High Peak. Once a forest fire had swept the mountain. The highest point was still bare, and from there one had a seven-mile outlook. He saw valleys and lakes, dark forest tracts and flourishing towns, churches and manors, little woodland crofts and large villages. Far in the distance lay the city, enveloped in a white haze from which a pair of gleaming spires peeped out. Public roads wound through the valleys, and a railway train was rushing along the border of the forest. It was a whole kingdom that he saw.

He flung himself upon the ground, all the while keeping his eyes riveted upon the vast outlook. There was something grand and majestic about the landscape before him, which made him feel himself and his sorrows small and insignificant.

He remembered how, when a child, he had read that the tempter led Jesus up to a high mountain and showed him all the world's glories, and he always fancied that they had stood up here on Great Peak, and he repeated the old words: "All these things will I give thee if thou wilt fall down and worship me."

All of a sudden he was thinking that a similar

temptation had come to him these last days. Certainly the tempter had not borne him to a high mountain and shown him all the glories and powers of this world! "Only be silent about the evil which you think you have done," said he, "and I will give you all these things."

As Gudmund thought on this, a grain of satisfaction came to him. "I have answered no," he said, and suddenly he understood what it had meant for him. If he had kept silent, would he not have been compelled to worship the tempter all his life? He would have been a timid and faint-hearted man; simply a slave to his possessions. The fear of discovery would always have weighed upon him. Nevermore would he have felt himself a free man.

A great peace came over Gudmund. He was happy in the consciousness that he had done right. When he thought back to the past days, he felt that he had groped his way out of a great darkness. It was wonderful that he had come out right finally. He asked himself how he had ever happened to go astray. "It was because they were so kind to me at home," he thought, "and the best help was that Helga came and wished me happiness."

He lay up there on the mountain a little longer, but presently he felt that he must go home to his father and mother and tell them that he was at peace with himself. When he rose to go, he saw Helga sitting on a ledge a little farther down the mountain.

Where she sat, she had not the big, broad outlook which he enjoyed; only a little glint of the valley was visible to her. This was in the direction where Närlunda lay, and possibly she could see a portion of the farm. When Gudmund discovered her, he felt that his heart, which all the day before had labored heavily and anxiously, began to beat lightly and merrily; at the same time such a thrill of joy ran through him that he stood still and marvelled at himself. "What has come over me? What is this?" he wondered, as the blood surged through his body and happiness gripped him with a force that was almost painful. At last he said to himself in a surprised tone: "Why, it is she that I'm fond of! Think, that I did not know it until now!"

It took hold of him with the strength of a loosened torrent. He had been bound the whole time he knew her. All that had drawn him to her he had held back. Now, at last, he was freed from the thought of marrying some one else — free to love her.

"Helga!" he cried, rushing down the steep to

her. She turned round with a terrified shriek.
"Don't be frightened! It is only I."

"But are you not at church being married?"

"No, indeed! There will be no wedding to-
day. She does n't want me — she — Hildur."

Helga rose. She placed her hand on her heart
and closed her eyes. At that moment she must
have thought it was not Gudmund who had come.
It must be that her eyes and ears were bewitched
in the forest. Yet it was sweet and dear of him
to come, if only in a vision! She closed her eyes
and stood motionless to keep this vision a few
seconds longer.

Gudmund was wild and dizzy from the great
love that had flamed up in him. As soon as he
came down to Helga, he threw his arms around
her and kissed her, and she let it happen, for she
was absolutely stupefied with surprise. It was
too wonderful to believe that he, who should
now be standing in church beside his bride,
actually could have come here to the forest.
This phantom or ghost of him that had come to
her may as well kiss her.

But while Gudmund was kissing Helga, she
awoke and pushed him from her. She began to
shower him with questions. Was it really he?
What was he doing in the forest? Had any misfortune happened to him? Why was the wedding

postponed? Was Hildur ill? Did the clergy-man have a stroke in church?

Gudmund had not wished to talk to her of anything in the world save his love, but she forced him to tell her what had occurred. While he was speaking she sat still and listened with rapt attention.

She did not interrupt him until he mentioned the broken blade. Then she leaped up suddenly and asked if it was his clasp-knife, the one he had when she served with them.

"Yes, it was just that one," said he.

"How many blades were broken off?" she asked.

"Only one," he answered.

Then Helga's head began working. She sat with knit brows trying to recall something. Wait! Why, certainly she remembered distinctly that she had borrowed the knife from him to shave wood with the day before she left. She had broken it then, but she had never told him of it. He had avoided her, and at that time he had not wished to hold any converse with her. And of course the knife had been in his pocket ever since and he had n't noticed that it was broken.

She raised her head and was about to tell him of this, but he went on talking of his visit that

6

morning to the house where the wedding was to
have been celebrated, and she wanted to let him
finish. When she heard how he had parted from
Hildur, she thought it such a terrible misfortune
that she began upbraiding him. "This is your
own fault," said she. "You and your father
came and frightened the life out of her with the
shocking news. She would not have answered
thus had she been mistress of herself. I want to
say to you that I believe she regrets it at this
very moment."

"Let her regret it as much as she likes, for all
of me!" said Gudmund. "I know now that
she is the sort who thinks only of herself. I am
glad I 'm rid of her!"

Helga pressed her lips, as if to keep the great
secret from escaping. There was much for her to
think about. It was more than a question of
clearing Gudmund of the murder; the wretched
affair had also dragged with it enmity between
Gudmund and his sweetheart. Perhaps she
might try to adjust this matter with the help
of what she knew.

Again she sat silent and pondered until Gudmund began telling that he had transferred his
affections to her.

But to her this seemed to be the greatest misfortune he had met with that day. It was bad

that he was about to miss the advantageous marriage, but still worse were he to woo a girl like herself. "No, such things you must not say to me," she said, rising abruptly.

"Why should n't I say this to you?" asked Gudmund, turning pale. "Perhaps it is with you as with Hildur — you are afraid of me?"

"No, that 's not the reason."

She wanted to explain how he was seeking his own ruin, but he was not listening to her. "I have heard said that there were women-folk in olden times who stood side by side with men when they were in trouble; but that kind one does not encounter nowadays."

A tremor passed through Helga. She could have thrown her arms around his neck, but remained perfectly still. To-day it was she who must be sensible.

"True, I should not have asked you to become my wife on the day that I must go to prison. You see, if I only knew that you would wait for me until I 'm free again, I should go through all the hardship with courage. Every one will now regard me as a criminal, as one who drinks and murders. If only there were some one who could think of me with affection! — this would sustain me more than anything else."

"You know, surely, that I shall never think anything but good of you, Gudmund."

Helga was so still! Gudmund's entreaties were becoming almost too much for her. She did n't know how she should escape him. He apprehended nothing of this, but began thinking he had been mistaken. She could not feel toward him as he did toward her. He came very close and looked at her, as though he wanted to look through her. "Are you not sitting on this particular ledge of the mountain that you may look down to Närlunda?"

"Yes."

"Don't you long night and day to be there?"

"Yes, but I 'm not longing for any person."

"And you don't care for me?"

"Yes, but I don't want to marry you."

"Whom do you care for, then?"

Helga was silent.

"Is it Per Mårtensson?"

"I have already told you that I liked him," she said, exhausted by the strain of it all.

Gudmund stood for a moment, with tense features, and looked at her. "Farewell, then! Now we must go our separate ways, you and I," said he. With that he made a long jump from this ledge of the mountain down to the next landing and disappeared among the trees.

VI

GUDMUND was hardly out of sight when Helga
rushed down the mountain in another direction.
She ran past the marsh without stopping and
hurried over the wooded hills as fast as she could
and down the road. She stopped at the first
farmhouse she came to and asked for the loan of
a horse and car to drive to Älvåkra. She said
that it was a matter of life and death and promised to pay for the help. The church folk had
already returned to their homes and were talking
of the adjourned wedding. They were all very
much excited and very solicitous and were eager
to help Helga, since she appeared to have an
important errand to the home of the bride.

At Älvåkra Hildur Ericsdotter sat in a little
room on the upper floor where she had dressed
as a bride. Her mother and several other peasant women were with her. Hildur did not weep;
she was unusually quiet, and so pale that she
looked as though she might be ill at any moment.
The women talked all the while of Gudmund.
All blamed him and seemed to regard it as a
fortunate thing that she was rid of him. Some
thought that Gudmund had shown very little
consideration for his parents-in-law in not letting them know on Palm Sunday how matters

stood with him. Others, again, said that one
who had had such happiness awaiting him
should have known how to take better care of
himself. A few congratulated Hildur because
she had escaped marrying a man who could
drink himself so full that he did not know what
he was doing.

Amid this, Hildur was losing her patience and
rose to go out. As soon as she was outside the
door, her best friend, a young peasant girl, came
and whispered something to her. "There is
some one below who wants to speak with you."

"Is it Gudmund?" asked Hildur, and a spark
of life came into her eyes.

"No, but it may be a messenger from him.
She would n't divulge the nature of her errand
to any one but yourself, she declared."

Hildur had been sitting thinking all day that
some one must come who could put an end to
her misery. She could n't comprehend that
such a dreadful misfortune should come to her.
She felt that something ought to happen that
she might again don her crown and wreath, so
they could proceed with the wedding. When
she heard now of a messenger from Gudmund,
she was interested and immediately went out
to the kitchen hall and looked for her.

Hildur probably wondered why Gudmund

had sent Helga to her, but she thought that perhaps he could n't find any other messenger on a holiday, and greeted her pleasantly. She motioned to Helga to come with her into the dairy across the yard. "I know no other place where we can be alone," she said. "The house is still full of guests."

As soon as they were inside, Helga went close up to Hildur and looked her square in the face. "Before I say anything more, I must know if you love Gudmund."

Hildur winced. It was painful for her to be obliged to exchange a single word with Helga, and she had no desire to make a confidant of her. But now it was a case of necessity, and she forced herself to answer, "Why else do you suppose I wished to marry him?"

"I mean, do you still love him?"

Hildur was like stone, but she could not lie under the other woman's searching glance. "Perhaps I have never loved him so much as to-day," she said, but she said this so feebly that one might think it hurt her to speak out.

"Then come with me at once!" said Helga. "I have a wagon down the road. Go in after a cloak or something to wrap around you; then we'll drive to Närlunda."

"What good would it do for me to go there?" asked Hildur.

"You must go there and say you want to be Gudmund's, no matter what he may have done, and that you will wait faithfully for him while he is in prison."

"Why should I say this?"

"So all will be well between you."

"But that is impossible. I don't want to marry any one who has been in prison!"

Helga staggered back, as though she had bumped against a wall, but she quickly regained her courage. She could understand that one who was rich and powerful, like Hildur, must think thus. "I should not come and ask you to go to Närlunda did I not know that Gudmund was innocent," said she.

Now it was Hildur who came a step or two towards Helga. "Do you know this for certain, or is it only something which you imagine?"

"It will be better for us to get into the cart immediately; then I can talk on the way."

"No, you must first explain what you mean; I must know what I'm doing."

Helga was in such a fever of excitement that she could hardly stand still; nevertheless she had to make up her mind to tell Hildur how she happened to know that Gudmund was not the murderer.

"Did n't you tell Gudmund of this at once?"

"No, I'm telling it now to Hildur. No one else knows of it."

"And why do you come to me with this?"

"That all may be well between you two. He will soon learn that he has done no wrong; but I want you to go to him as if of your own accord, and make it up."

"Sha'n't I say that I know he is innocent?"

"You must come entirely of your own accord and must never let him know I have spoken to you; otherwise he will never forgive you for what you said to him this morning."

Hildur listened quietly. There was something in this which she had never met with in her life before, and she was striving to make it clear to herself. "Do you know that it was I who wanted you to leave Närlunda?"

"I know, of course, that it was not the folk at Närlunda who wished me away."

"I can't comprehend that you should come to me to-day with the desire to help me."

"Only come along now, Hildur, so all will be well!"

Hildur stared at Helga, trying all the while to reason it out. "Perhaps Gudmund loves you?" she blurted out.

And now Helga's patience was exhausted. "What could I be to him?" she said sharply. "You know, Hildur, that I am only a poor croft girl, and that's not the worst about me!"

The two young women stole unobserved from the homestead and were soon seated in the cart. Helga held the reins, and she did not spare the horse, but drove at full speed. Both girls were silent. Hildur sat gazing at Helga. She marvelled at her and was thinking more of her than of anything else.

As they were nearing the Erlandsson farm, Helga gave the reins to Hildur. "Now you must go alone to the house and talk with Gudmund. I'll follow a little later and tell that about the knife. But you must n't say a word to Gudmund about my having brought you here."

Gudmund sat in the living-room at Närlunda beside his mother and talked with her. His father was sitting a little way from them, smoking. He looked pleased and said not a word. It was apparent that he thought everything was going now as it should and that it was not necessary for him to interfere.

"I wonder, mother, what you would have said if you had got Helga for a daughter-in-law?" ventured Gudmund.

Mother Ingeborg raised her head and said in a firm voice, "I will with pleasure welcome any daughter-in-law if I only know that she loves you as a wife should love her husband."

This was barely spoken when they saw Hildur Ericsdotter drive into the yard. She came immediately into the cottage and was unlike herself in many respects. She did not step into the room with her usual briskness, but it appeared almost as though she were inclined to pause near the door, like some poor beggar-woman.

However, she came forward finally and shook hands with mother Ingeborg and Erland. Then she turned to Gudmund: "It is with you that I would have a word or two."

Gudmund arose, and they went into the side room. He arranged a chair for Hildur, but she did not seat herself. She blushed with embarrassment, and the words dropped slowly and heavily from her lips. "I was — yes, it was much too hard — that which I said to you this morning."

"We came so abruptly, Hildur," said Gudmund.

She grew still more red and embarrassed. "I should have thought twice. We could — it would of course — "

"It is probably best as it is, Hildur. It is nothing to speak of now, but it was kind of you to come."

She put her hands to her face, drew a breath as deep as a sigh, then raised her head again.

"No!" she said, "I can't do it in this way. I don't want you to think that I'm better than I am. There was some one who came to me and told me that you were not guilty and advised me to hurry over here at once and make everything right again. And I was not to mention that I already knew you were innocent, for then you wouldn't think it so noble of me to come. Now I want to say to you that I wish I had thought of this myself, but I hadn't. But I have longed for you all day and wished that all might be well between us. Whichever way it turns out, I want to say that I am glad you are innocent."

"Who advised you to do this?" asked Gudmund.

"I was not to tell you that."

"I am surprised that any one should know of it. Father has but just returned from the Sheriff. He telegraphed to the city, and an answer has come that the real murderer has already been found."

As Gudmund was relating this, Hildur felt

that her legs were beginning to shake, and she sat down quickly in the chair. She was frightened because Gudmund was so calm and pleasant, and she was beginning to perceive that he was wholly out of her power. "I can understand that you can never forget how I behaved to you this forenoon."

"Surely I can forgive you that," he said in the same even tone. "We will never speak of the matter again."

She shivered, dropped her eyes, and sat as though she were expecting something. "It was simply a stroke of good fortune, Hildur," he said, coming forward and grasping her hand, "that it is over between us, for to-day it became clear to me that I love another. I think I have been fond of her for a long time, but I did not know it until to-day."

"Whom do you care for, Gudmund?" came in a colorless voice from Hildur.

"It does n't matter. I shall not marry her, as she does not care for me, nor can I marry anyone else."

Hildur raised her head. It was not easy to tell what was taking place in her. At this moment she felt that she, the rich farmer's daughter, with all her beauty and all her possessions, was nothing to Gudmund. She was proud and did not wish to part from him without teaching him that she had a value of her own, apart from all the external things. "I want you to tell me, Gudmund, if it is Helga from Big Marsh whom you love."

Gudmund was silent.

"It was she who came to me and taught me what I should do that all might be well between us. She knew you were innocent, but she did not say so to you. She let me know it first."

Gudmund looked her steadily in the eyes. "Do you think this means that she has a great affection for me?"

"You may be sure of it, Gudmund. I can prove it. No one in the world could love you more than she does."

He walked rapidly across the floor and back, then he stopped suddenly before Hildur. "And you — why do you tell me this?"

"Surely I do not wish to stand beneath Helga in magnanimity!"

"Oh, Hildur, Hildur!" he cried, placing his hands on her shoulders and shaking her to give vent to his emotion. "You don't know, oh, you don't know how much I like you at this moment! You don't know how happy you have made me!"

Helga sat by the roadside and waited. With

her cheek resting on her hand, she sat and
pictured Hildur and Gudmund together and
thought how happy they must be now.

While she sat thus, a servant from Närlunda
came along. He stopped when he saw her. "I
suppose you have heard that affair which concerns Gudmund?"

She had.

"It was not true, fortunately. The real murderer is already in custody."

"I knew it could n't be true," said Helga.

Thereupon the man went, and Helga sat there
alone, as before. So they knew it already down
there! It was not necessary for her to go to
Närlunda and tell of it.

She felt herself so strangely shut out! Earlier
in the day she had been so eager. She had not
thought of herself — only that Gudmund and
Hildur's marriage should take place. But now
it flashed upon her how alone she was. And it
was hard not to be something to those of whom
one is fond. Gudmund did not need her now,
and her own child had been appropriated by her
mother, who would hardly allow her to look at it.

She was thinking that she had better rise and
go home, but the hills appeared long and difficult to her. She did n't know how she should
ever be able to climb them.

A vehicle came along now from the direction of Närlunda. Hildur and Gudmund were seated in the cart. Now they were probably on their way to Älväkra to tell that they were reconciled. To-morrow the wedding would take place.

When they discovered Helga, they stopped the horse. Gudmund handed the reins to Hildur and jumped down. Hildur nodded to Helga and drove on.

Gudmund remained standing on the road and facing Helga. "I am glad you are sitting here, Helga," he said. "I thought that I would have to go up to Big Marsh to meet you."

He said this abruptly, almost harshly; at the same time he gripped her hand tightly. And she read in his eyes that he knew now where he had her. Now she could no more escape from him.

The Silver Mine

The Silver Mine

KING GUSTAF THE THIRD was travelling through Dalecarlia. He was pressed for time, and all the way he wanted to drive like lightning. Although they drove with such speed that the horses were extended like stretched rubber bands and the coach cleared the turns on two wheels, the King poked his head out of the window and shouted to the postilion: "Why don't you go ahead? Do you think you are driving over eggs?"

Since they had to drive over poor country roads at such a mad pace, it would have been almost a miracle had the harness and wagon held together! And they did n't, either; for at the foot of a steep hill the pole broke — and there the King sat! The courtiers sprang from the coach and scolded the driver, but this did not lessen the damage done. There was no possibility of continuing the journey until the coach was mended.

When the courtiers looked round to try and find something with which the King could amuse himself while he waited, they noticed a church spire looming high above the trees in a grove a short distance ahead. They intimated to the King that he might step into one of the coaches in which the attendants were riding and drive up to the church. It was a Sunday, and the King might attend service to pass the time until the royal coach was ready.

The King accepted the proposal and drove toward the church. He had been travelling for hours through dark forest regions, but here it looked more cheerful, with fairly large meadows and villages, and with the Dal River gliding on, light and pretty, between thick rows of alder bushes.

But the King had ill-luck to this extent: the bellringer took up the recessional chant just as the King was stepping from the coach on the church knoll and the people were coming out from the service. But when they came walking past him, the King remained standing, with one foot in the wagon and the other on the footstep. He did not move from the spot — only stared at them. They were the finest lot of folk he had ever seen. All the men were above the average height, with intelligent and earnest faces, and the women were dignified and stately, with an air of Sabbath peace about them.

The whole of the preceding day the King had talked only of the desolate tracts he was passing through, and had said to his courtiers again and again, "Now I am certainly driving through the very poorest part of my kingdom!" But now, when he saw the people, garbed in the picturesque dress of this section of the country, he forgot to think of their poverty; instead his heart warmed, and he remarked to himself: "The King of Sweden is not so badly off as his enemies think. So long as my subjects look like this, I shall probably be able to defend both my faith and my country."

He commanded the courtiers to make known to the people that the stranger who was standing amongst them was their King, and that they should gather around him, so he could talk to them.

And then the King made a speech to the people. He spoke from the high steps outside the vestry, and the narrow step upon which he stood is there even to-day.

The King gave an account of the sad plight in which the kingdom was placed. He said that the Swedes were threatened with war, both by Russians and Danes. Under ordinary circumstances it would n't be such a serious matter, but now the army was filled with traitors, and he did not dare depend upon it. Therefore there was no other course for him to pursue than to go himself into the country settlements and ask his subjects if they would be loyal to their King and help him with men and money, so he could save the Fatherland.

The peasants stood quietly while the King was speaking, and when he had finished they gave no sign either of approval or disapproval.

The King himself thought that he had spoken very well. The tears had sprung to his eyes several times while he was speaking. But when the peasants stood there all the while, troubled and undecided, and could not make up their minds to answer him, the King frowned and looked displeased.

The peasants understood that it was becoming monotonous for the King to wait, and finally one of them stepped out from the crowd.

"Now, you must know, King Gustaf, that we were not expecting a royal visit in the parish to-day," said the peasant, "and therefore we are not prepared to answer you at once. I advise you to go into the vestry and speak with our pastor, while we discuss among ourselves this matter which you have laid before us."

The King apprehended that a more satisfactory response was not to be had immediately, so he felt that it would be best for him to follow the peasant's advice.

When he came into the vestry, he found no one there but a man who looked like a peasant. He was tall and rugged, with big hands, toughened by labor, and he wore neither cassock nor collar, but leather breeches and a long white homespun coat, like all the other men

He arose and bowed to the King when the latter entered.

"I thought I should find the parson in here," said the King.

The man grew somewhat red in the face. He thought it annoying to mention the fact that he was the parson of this parish, when he saw that the King had mistaken him for a peasant. "Yes," said he, "the parson is usually on hand in here."

The King dropped into a large armchair which stood in the vestry at that time, and which stands there to-day, looking exactly like itself, with this difference: the congregation has had a gilded crown attached to the back of it.

"Have you a good parson in this parish?" asked the King, who wanted to appear interested in the welfare of the peasants.

When the King questioned him in this manner,

the parson felt that he could n't possibly tell who he was. "It's better to let him go on believing that I'm only a peasant," thought he, and replied that the parson was good enough. He preached a pure and clear gospel and tried to live as he taught.

The King thought that this was a good commendation, but he had a sharp ear and marked a certain doubt in the tone. "You sound as if you were not quite satisfied with the parson," said the King.

"He's a bit arbitrary," said the man, thinking that if the King should find out later who he was, he would not think that the parson had been standing here and blowing his own horn, therefore he wished to come out with a little fault-finding also. "There are some, no doubt, who say the parson wants to be the only one to counsel and rule in this parish," he continued.

"Then, at all events, he has led and managed in the best possible way," said the King. He did n't like it that the peasant complained of one who was placed above him. "To me it appears as though good habits and old-time simplicity were the rule here."

"The people are good enough," said the curate, "but then they live in poverty and isolation. Human beings here would certainly be no better than others if this world's temptations came closer to them."

"But there's no fear of anything of the sort happening," said the King with a shrug.

He said nothing further, but began thrumming on the table with his fingers. He thought he had exchanged a sufficient number of gracious words with this peasant and wondered when the others would be ready with their answer.

"These peasants are not very eager to help their King," thought he. "If I only had my coach, I would drive away from them and their palaver!"

The pastor sat there troubled, debating with himself as to how he should decide an important matter which he must settle. He was beginning to feel happy because he had not told the King who he was. Now he felt that he could speak with him about matters which otherwise he could not have placed before him.

After a while the parson broke the silence and asked the King if it was an actual fact that enemies were upon them and that the kingdom was in danger.

The King thought this man ought to have sense enough not to trouble him further. He simply glared at him and said nothing.

"I ask because I was standing in here and

could not hear very well," said the parson. "But if this is really the case, I want to say to you that the pastor of this congregation might perhaps be able to procure for the King as much money as he will need."

"I thought you said just now that every one here was poor," said the King, thinking that the man did n't know what he was talking about.

"Yes, that is true," replied the rector, "and the parson has no more than any of the others. But if the King would condescend to listen to me for a moment, I will explain how the pastor happens to have the power to help him."

"You may speak," said the King. "You seem to find it easier to get the words past your lips than your friends and neighbors out there, who never will be ready with what they have to tell me."

"It is not so easy to reply to the King! I 'm afraid that, in the end, it will be the parson who must undertake this on behalf of the others."

The King crossed his legs, folded his arms, and let his head sink down on his breast. "You may begin now," he said in the tone of one already asleep.

"Once upon a time there were five men from this parish who were out on a moose hunt," began the clergyman. "One of them was the parson of whom we are speaking. Two of the others were soldiers, named Olaf and Eric Svärd; the fourth man was the innkeeper in this settlement, and the fifth was a peasant named Israel Per Persson."

"Don't go to the trouble of mentioning so many names," muttered the King, letting his head droop to one side.

"Those men were good hunters," continued the parson, "who usually had luck with them; but that day they had wandered long and far without getting anything. Finally they gave up the hunt altogether and sat down on the ground to talk. They said there was not a spot in the whole forest fit for cultivation; all of it was only mountain and swamp land. 'Our Lord has not done right by us in giving us such a poor land to live in,' said one. 'In other localities people can get riches for themselves in abundance, but here, with all our toil and drudgery, we can scarcely get our daily bread.'"

The pastor paused a moment, as if uncertain that the King heard him, but the latter moved his little finger to show that he was awake.

"Just as the hunters were discussing this matter, the parson saw something that glittered at the base of the mountain, where he had kicked away a moss-tuft. 'This is a queer mountain,' he thought, as he kicked off another moss-tuft. He picked up a shiver of stone that came with the moss and which shone exactly like the other. 'It can't be possible that this stuff is lead,' said he. Then the others sprang up and scraped away the turf with the butt end of their rifles. When they did this, they saw plainly that a broad vein of ore followed the mountain. 'What do you think this might be?' asked the parson. The men chipped off bits of stone and bit into them. 'It must be lead, or zinc at least,' said they. 'And the whole mountain is full of it,' added the innkeeper."

When the parson had got thus far in his narrative, the King's head was seen to straighten up a little and one eye opened. "Do you know if any of those persons knew anything about ore and minerals?" he asked.

"They did not," replied the parson.

Then the King's head sank and both eyes closed.

"The clergyman and his companions were very happy," continued the speaker, without letting himself be disturbed by the King's indifference; "they fancied that now they had found that which would give them and their descendants wealth. 'I'll never have to do any more work,' said one. 'Now I can afford to do nothing at all the whole week through, and on Sundays I shall drive to church in a golden chariot!' They were otherwise sensible men, but the great find had gone to their heads and they talked like children. Still they had enough presence of mind to put back the moss-tufts and conceal the vein of ore. Then they carefully noted the place where it was, and went home. Before they parted company, they agreed that the parson should travel to Falun and ask the mining expert what kind of ore this was. He was to return as soon as possible, and until then they promised one another on oath not to reveal to a single soul where the ore was to be found."

The King's head was raised again a trifle, but he did not interrupt the speaker with a word. It appeared as though he was beginning to believe that the man actually had something of importance he wished to say to him, since he did n't allow himself to be disturbed by his indifference.

"Then the parson departed with a few samples of ore in his pocket. He was just as happy in the thought of becoming rich as the others were. He was thinking of rebuilding the parsonage, which at present was no better than a peasant's cottage, and then he would marry a dean's daughter whom he liked. He had thought that he might have to wait for her many years!

He was poor and obscure and knew that it would be a long while before he should get any post that would enable him to marry.

"The parson drove over to Falun in two days, and there he had to wait another whole day because the mining expert was away. Finally, he ran across him and showed him the bits of ore. The mining expert took them in his hand. He looked at them first, then at the parson. The parson related how he had found them in a mountain at home in his parish, and wondered if it might not be lead.

"'No, it 's not lead,' said the mining expert.

"'Perhaps it is zinc, then?' asked the parson.

"'Nor is it zinc,' said the mineralogist.

"The parson thought that all the hope within him sank. He had not been so depressed in many a long day.

"'Have you many stones like these in your parish?' asked the mineralogist.

"'We have a whole mountain full,' said the parson.

"Then the mineralogist came up closer, slapped the parson on the shoulder, and said, 'Let us see that you make such good use of this that it will prove a blessing both to yourselves and to the country, for this is silver.'

"'Indeed?' said the parson, feeling his way. 'So it is silver!'

"The mineralogist began telling him how he should go to work to get legal rights to the mine and gave him many valuable suggestions; but the parson stood there dazed and did n't listen to what he was saying. He was only thinking of how wonderful it was that at home in his poor parish stood a whole mountain of silver ore, waiting for him."

The King raised his head so suddenly that the parson stopped short in his narrative. "It turned out, of course, that when he got home and began working the mine, he saw that the mineralogist had only been stringing him," said the King.

"Oh, no, the mineralogist had not fooled him," said the parson.

"You may continue," said the King, as he settled himself more comfortably in the chair to listen.

"When the parson was at home again and was driving through the parish," continued the clergyman, "he thought that first of all he should inform his partners of the value of their find. And as he drove alongside the innkeeper Sten Stensson's place, he intended to drive up to the house to tell him they had found silver.

But when he stopped outside the gate, he noticed that a broad path of evergreen was strewn all the way up to the doorstep.

"'Who has died in this place?' asked the parson of a boy who stood leaning against the fence.

"'The innkeeper himself,' answered the boy. Then he let the clergyman know that the innkeeper had drunk himself full every day for a week. 'Oh, so much brandy, so much brandy has been drunk here!'

"'How can that be?' asked the parson. 'The innkeeper used never to drink himself full.'

"'Oh,' said the boy, 'he drank because he said he had found a mine. He was very rich. He should never have to do anything now but drink, he said. Last night he drove off, full as he was, and the wagon turned over and he was killed.'

"When the parson heard this, he drove homeward. He was distressed over what he had heard. He had come back so happy, rejoicing because he could tell the great good news.

"When the parson had driven a few paces, he saw Israel Per Persson walking along. He looked about as usual, and the parson thought it was well that fortune had not gone to his head too. Him he would cheer at once with the news that he was a rich man.

"'Good day!' said Per Persson. 'Do you come from Falun now?'

_"'I do,' said the parson. 'And now I must tell you that it has turned out even better than we had imagined. The mineralogist said it was silver ore that we had found.'

"That instant Per Persson looked as though the ground under him had opened! 'What are you saying, what are you saying? Is it silver?'

"'Yes,' answered the parson. 'We'll all be rich men now, all of us, and can live like gentlemen.'

"'Oh, is it silver!' said Per Persson once again, looking more and more mournful.

"'Why, of course it is silver,' replied the parson. 'You must n't think that I want to deceive you. You must n't be afraid of being happy.'

"'Happy!' said Per Persson. 'Should I be happy? I believed it was only glitter that we had found, so I thought it would be better to take the certain for the uncertain: I have sold my share in the mine to Olaf Svärd for a hundred dollars.' He was desperate, and when the parson drove away from him, he stood on the highway and wept.

"When the clergyman got back to his home, he sent a servant to Olaf Svärd and his brother to tell them that it was silver they had found. He thought that he had had quite enough of driving around and spreading the good news.

"But in the evening, when the parson sat alone, his joy asserted itself again. He went out in the darkness and stood on a hillock upon which he contemplated building the new parsonage. It should be imposing, of course, as fine as a bishop's palace.. He stood out there long that night; nor did he content himself with rebuilding the parsonage! It occurred to him that, since there were such riches to be found in the parish, throngs of people would pour in and, finally, a whole city would be built around the mine. And then he would have to erect a new church in place of the old one. Towards this object a large portion of his wealth would probably go. And he was not content with this, either, but fancied that when his church was ready, the King and many bishops would come to the dedication. Then the King would be pleased with the church, but he would remark that there was no place where a king might put up, and then he would have to erect a castle in the new city."

Just then one of the King's courtiers opened the door of the vestry and announced that the big royal coach was mended.

At the first moment the King was ready to withdraw, but on second thought he changed his mind. "You may tell your story to the end," he said to the parson. "But you can hurry it a bit. We know all about how the man thought and dreamed. We want to know how he acted."

"But while the parson was still lost in his dreams," continued the clergyman, "word came to him that Israel Per Persson had made away with himself. He had not been able to bear the disappointment of having sold his share in the mine. He had thought, no doubt, that he could not endure to go about every day seeing another enjoying the wealth that might have been his."

The King straightened up a little. He kept both eyes open. "Upon my word," he said, "if I had been that parson, I should have had enough of the mine!"

"The King is a rich man," said the parson. "He has quite enough, at all events. It is not the same thing with a poor curate who possesses nothing. The unhappy wretch thought instead, when he saw that God's blessing was not with his enterprise: 'I will dream no more of bringing glory and profit to myself with these riches; but I can't let the silver lie buried in the earth! I must take it out, for the benefit of the poor and needy. I will work the mine, to put the whole parish on its feet.'

"So one day the parson went out to see Olaf Svärd, to ask him and his brother as to what should be done immediately with the silver mountain. When he came in the vicinity of the barracks, he met a cart surrounded by armed peasants, and in the cart sat a man with his hands tied behind him and a rope around his ankles.

"When the parson passed by, the cart stopped, and he had time to regard the prisoner, whose head was tied up so it was n't easy to see who he was. But the parson thought he recognized Olaf Svärd. He heard the prisoner beg those who guarded him to let him speak a few words with the parson.

"The parson drew nearer, and the prisoner turned toward him. 'You will soon be the only one who knows where the silver mine is,' said Olaf.

"'What are you saying, Olaf?' asked the parson.

"'Well, you see, parson, since we have learned that it was a silver mine we had found, my brother and I could no longer be as good friends as before. We were continually quarrelling. Last night we got into a controversy over which one of us five it was who first discovered the mine. It ended in strife between us, and we came to blows. I have killed my brother and he has left me with a souvenir across the forehead to remember him by. I must hang now, and then you will be the only one who knows anything about the mine; therefore I wish to ask something of you.'

"'Speak out!' said the parson. 'I'll do what I can for you.'

"'You know that I am leaving several little children behind me,' began the soldier, but the parson interrupted him.

"'As regards this, you can rest easy. That which comes to your share in the mine, they shall have, exactly as if you yourself were living.'

"'No,' said Olaf Svärd, 'it was another thing I wanted to ask of you. Don't let them have any portion of that which comes from the mine!'

"The parson staggered back a step. He stood there dumb and could not answer.

"'If you do not promise me this, I cannot die in peace,' said the prisoner.

"'Yes,' said the parson slowly and painfully. 'I promise you what you ask of me.'

"Thereupon the murderer was taken away, and the parson stood on the highway thinking how he should keep the promise he had given him. On the way home he thought of the wealth which he had been so happy over. But if it really were true that the people in this community could not stand riches? — Already four were ruined, who hitherto had been dignified and excellent men. He seemed to see the whole community before him, and he pictured to himself how this silver mine would destroy one after another. Was it befitting that he, who had been appointed to watch over these poor human beings' souls, should let loose upon them that which would be their destruction?"

All of a sudden the King sat bolt upright in his chair. "I declare!" said he, "you'll make me understand that a parson in this isolated settlement must be every inch a man."

"Nor was it enough with what had already happened," continued the parson, "for as soon as the news about the mine spread among the parishioners, they stopped working and went about in idleness, waiting for the time when great riches should pour in on them. All the ne'er-do-wells there were in this section streamed in, and drunkenness and fighting were what the parson heard talked of continually. A lot of people did nothing but tramp round in the forest searching for the mine, and the parson marked that as soon as he left the house people

followed him stealthily to find out if he was n't
going to the silver mountain and to steal the
secret from him.

"When matters were come to this pass, the
parson called the peasants together to vote.
To start with, he reminded them of all the mis-
fortunes which the discovery of the mountain
had brought upon them, and he asked them if
they were going to let themselves be ruined or
if they would save themselves. Then he told
them that they must not expect him, who was
their spiritual adviser, to help on their destruction. Now he had decided not to reveal to any
one where the silver mine was, and never would
he himself take riches from it. And then he
asked the peasants how they would have it
henceforth. If they wished to continue their
search for the mine and wait upon riches, then
he would go so far away that not a hearsay of
their misery could reach him; but if they would
give up thinking about the silver mine and be as
heretofore, he would remain with them. 'Whichever way you may choose,' said the parson, 'remember this, that from me no one shall ever
know anything about the silver mountain!'"

"Well," said the King, "how did they decide?"

"They did as their pastor wished," said the

parson. "They understood that he meant well
by them when he wanted to remain poor for
their sakes. And they commissioned him to go
to the forest and conceal the vein of ore with
evergreen and stone, so that no one would be
able to find it — neither they themselves nor
their posterity."

"And ever since the parson has been living
here just as poor as the rest?"

"Yes," answered the curate, "he has lived
here just as poor as the rest."

"He has married, of course, and built himself
a new parsonage?" said the King.

"No, he could n't afford to marry, and he
lives in the old cabin."

"It 's a pretty story that you have told me,"
said the King. After a few seconds he resumed:
"Was it of the silver mountain that you were
thinking when you said that the parson here
would be able to procure for me as much money
as I need?"

"Yes," said the other.

"But I can't put the thumb-screws on him,"
said the King. "Or how would you that I
should get such a man to show me the mountain — a man who has renounced his sweetheart and all the allurements of life?"

"Oh, that 's a different matter," said the

parson, "But if it's the Fatherland that is in need of the fortune, he will probably give in."

"Will you answer for that?" asked the King.

"Yes, that I will answer for," said the clergyman.

"Does n't he care, then, what becomes of his parishioners?"

"That can rest in God's hand."

The King rose from the chair and walked over to the window. He stood for a moment and looked upon the group of people outside. The longer he looked, the clearer his large eyes shone, and his figure seemed to grow. "You may greet the pastor of this congregation, and say that for Sweden's King there is no sight more beautiful than to see a people such as this!"

Then the King turned from the window and looked at the clergyman. He began to smile. "Is it true that the pastor of this parish is so poor that he removes his black clothes as soon as the service is over and dresses himself like a peasant?" asked the King.

"Yes, so poor is he," said the curate, and a crimson flush leaped into his rough-hewn face.

The King went back to the window. One could see that he was in his best mood. All that was noble and great within him had been quickened into life. "You must let that mine lie in peace," said the King. "Inasmuch as you have labored and starved a lifetime to make this people such as you would have it, you may keep it as it is."

"But if the kingdom is in danger?" said the parson.

"The kingdom is better served with men than with money," remarked the King. When had said this, he bade the clergyman farewell and went out from the vestry.

Without stood the group of people, as quiet and taciturn as they were when he went in. As the King came down the steps, a peasant stepped up to him.

"Have you had a talk with our pastor?" said the peasant.

"Yes," said the King. "I have talked with him."

"Then of course you have our answer?" said the peasant. "We asked you to go in and talk with our parson, that he might give you an answer from us."

"I have the answer," said the King.

The Airship

The Airship

FATHER and the boys are seated one rainy October evening in a third-class railway coach on their way to Stockholm. The father is sitting by himself on one bench, and the boys sit close together directly opposite him, reading a Jules Verne romance entitled "Six Weeks in a Balloon." The book is much worn. The boys know it almost by heart and have held endless discussions on it, but they always read it with the same pleasure. They have forgotten everything else to follow the daring sailors of the air all over Africa, and seldom raise their eyes from the book to glance at the Swedish towns they are travelling through.

The boys are very like each other. They are the same height, are dressed alike, with blue caps and gray overcoats, and both have large dreamy eyes and little pug noses. They are always good friends, always together, do not bother with other children, and are forever talking about inventions and exploring expeditions. In point of talent they are quite unlike. Lennart, the elder, who is thirteen, is backward in his studies at the High School and can hardly keep up with his class in any theme. To make up for this, he is very handy and enterprising. He is going to be an inventor and works all the time on a flying-machine which he is constructing. Hugo is a year younger than Lennart, but he is quicker at study and is already in the same grade as his brother. He does n't find studying any special fun, either; but, on the other hand, he is a great sportsman — a ski-runner, a cyclist, and a skater. He intends to start out on voyages of discovery when he is grown up. As soon as Lennart's airship is ready, Hugo is going to travel in it in order to explore what is still left of this globe to be discovered.

Their father is a tall thin man with a sunken chest, a haggard face, and pretty, slender hands. He is carelessly dressed. His shirt bosom is wrinkled and the coat band pokes up at the neck; his vest is buttoned wrongly and his socks sag down over his shoes. He wears his hair so long at the neck that it hangs on his coat collar. This is due not to carelessness, but to habit and taste.

The father is a descendant of an old musical family from far back in a rural district, and he has brought with him into the world two strong inclinations, one of which is a great musical talent; and it was this that first came into the light. He was graduated from the Academy in Stockholm and then studied a few years abroad, and during these study years made such brilliant progress that both he and his teacher thought he would some day be a great and world-renowned violinist. He certainly had talent enough to reach the goal, but he lacked grit and perseverance. He could n't fight his way to any sort of standing out in the world, but soon came home again and accepted a situation as organist in a country town. At the start he felt ashamed because he had not lived up to the expectations of every one, but he felt, also, that it was good to have an assured income and not be forced to depend any longer upon the charity of others.

Shortly after he had got the appointment, he married, and a few years later he was perfectly satisfied with his lot. He had a pretty little home, a cheerful and contented wife, and two little boys. He was the town favorite, fêted, and in great demand everywhere. But then there came a time when all this did not seem to satisfy him. He longed to go out in the world once more and try his luck; but he felt bound down at home because he had a wife and children.

More than all, it was the wife who had persuaded him to give up this journey. She had not believed that he would succeed any better now than before. She felt they were so happy that there was no need for him to strive after anything else. Unquestionably she made a mistake in this instance, but she also lived to regret it bitterly, for, from that time on, the other family trait showed itself. When his yearning for success and fame was not satisfied, he tried to console himself with drinking.

Now it turned out with him, as was usual with folk of his family — he drank inordinately. By degrees he became an entirely different person. He was no longer charming or lovable, but harsh and cruel; and the greatest misfortune of all was that he conceived a terrible hatred for his wife and tortured her in every conceivable way, both when he was drunk and when he was n't.

So the boys did not have a good home, and their childhood would have been very unhappy had they not been able to create for themselves a little world of their own, filled with machine models, exploring schemes, and books of adventure. The only one who has ever caught a glimpse of this world is the mother. The father has n't even a suspicion of its existence, nor can he talk with the boys about anything that interests them. He disturbs them, time and again,

by asking if they don't think it will be fun to see
Stockholm; if they are not glad to be out travelling with father, and other things in that way,
to which the boys give brief replies, in order that
they may immediately bury themselves in the
book again. Nevertheless the father continues
to question the boys. He thinks they are
charmed with his affability, although they are
too bashful to show it.

"They have been too long under petticoat
rule," he thinks. "They have become timid
and namby-pamby. There will be some go in
them now, when I take them in hand."

Father is mistaken. It is not because the boys
are bashful that they answer him so briefly; it
simply shows that they are well brought up and
do not wish to hurt his feelings. If they were
not polite, they would answer him in a very
different manner. "Why should we think it fun
to be travelling with father?" they would then
say. "Father must think himself something
wonderful, but we know, of course, that he is
only a poor wreck of a man. And why should
we be glad to see Stockholm? We understand
very well that it is not for our sakes that father
has taken us along, but only to make mother
unhappy!"

It would be wiser, no doubt, if the father

were to let the boys read without interrupting them. They are sad and apprehensive, and it irritates them to see him in a good humor. "It is only because he knows that mother is sitting at home crying that he is so happy to-day," they whisper to each other.

Father's questions finally bring matters to this pass: the boys read no more, although they continue to sit bent over the book. Instead, their thoughts begin in bitterness to embrace all that they have had to endure on their father's account.

They remember the time when he drank . himself full in the morning and came staggering up the street, with a crowd of school boys after him, who poked fun at him. They recall how the other boys teased them and gave them nick-names because they had a father who drank.

They have been put to shame for their father. They have been forced to live in a state of constant anxiety for his sake, and as soon as they were having any enjoyment, he always came and spoiled their fun. It is no small register of sins that they are setting down against him! The boys are very meek and patient, but they feel a greater and greater wrath springing up in them.

He should at least understand that, as yet,

they cannot forgive him for the great wrong he
did them yesterday. This was by far the worst
wrong he had ever done them.

It seems that, last year, mother and the boys
decided to part from father. For a number of
years he had been persecuting and torturing her
in every possible way, but she was loath to part
from him and remained, so that he would n't go
altogether to rack and ruin. But now, at last, she
wanted to do it for the sake of her boys. She
had noticed that their father made them unhappy, and realized that she must take them
away from this misery and provide them with
a good and peaceable home.

When the spring school-term was over, she sent
them to her parents in the country, and she herself went abroad in order to obtain a divorce in
the easiest way possible. She regretted that, by
going about it in this way, it would appear as
though it were her fault that the marriage was
dissolved; but that she must submit to. She was
even less pleased when the courts turned the boys
over to the father because she was a run-away
wife. She consoled herself with the thought that
he could n't possibly wish to keep the children;
but she had felt quite ill at ease.

As soon as the divorce was settled, she came
back and took a small apartment where she and

the boys were to live. In two days she had everything in readiness, so that they could come home to her.

It was the happiest day the boys had experienced. The entire apartment consisted of one large living-room and a big kitchen, but everything was new and pretty, and mother had arranged the place so cosily. The big room she and they were to use daytimes as a work-room, and nights they were to sleep there. The kitchen was light and comfortable. There they would eat, and in a little closet off the kitchen mother had her bed.

She had told them that they would be very poor. She had secured a place as singing-teacher at the girls' school, and this was all they had to live upon. They could n't afford to keep a servant, but must get along all by themselves. The boys were in ecstasies over everything — most of all, because they might help along. They volunteered to carry water and wood. They were to brush their own shoes and make their own beds. It was only fun to think up all that they were going to do!

There was a little wardrobe, in which Lennart was to keep all his mechanical apparatus. He was to have the key himself, and no one but Hugo and he should ever go in there.

But the boys were allowed to be happy with their mother only for a single day. Afterwards their father spoiled their pleasure, as he had always done as far back as they could remember. Mother told them she had heard that their father had received a legacy of a few thousand kronor, and that he had resigned from his position as organist and was going to move to Stockholm. Both they and mother were glad that he was leaving town, so they would escape meeting him on the streets. And then a friend of father's had called on mother to tell her that father wanted to take the boys with him to Stockholm.

Mother had wept and begged that she might keep her boys, but father's messenger had answered her that her husband was determined to have the boys under his guardianship. If they did not come willingly, he would let the police fetch them. He bade mother read through the divorce papers, and there it said plainly that the boys would belong to their father. This, of course, she already knew. It was not to be gainsaid.

Father's friend had said many nice things of father and had told her of how much he loved his sons, and for this reason he wanted them to be with him. But the boys knew that father was taking them away solely for the purpose of torturing mother. She would have to live in a state of continual anxiety for them. The whole thing was nothing but malice and revenge!

But father had his own way, and here they were now, on their way to Stockholm. And right opposite them their father sits, rejoicing in the thought that he has made their mother unhappy. With every second that passes, the thought of having to live with father becomes more repellent. Are they then wholly in his power? Will there be no help for this?

Father leans back in his seat, and after a bit he falls asleep. Immediately the boys begin whispering to each other very earnestly. It is n't difficult for them to come to a decision. The whole day they have been sitting there thinking that they ought to run away. They conclude to steal out on the platform and to jump from the train when it goes through a big forest. Then they will build them a hut in the most secluded spot in the forest, and live all by themselves and never show themselves to a human being.

While the boys are laying their plans, the train stops at a station, and a peasant woman, leading a little boy by the hand, comes into the coupé. She is dressed in black, with a shawl on her head, and has a kind and friendly appearance. She removes the little one's overcoat, which is wet from the rain, and wraps a shawl around him. Then she takes off his shoes and stockings, dries his little cold feet, takes from a bundle dry shoes and stockings and puts them on him. Then she gives him a stick of candy and lays him down on the seat with his head resting on her lap, that he might sleep.

First one boy, then the other casts a glance over at the peasant woman. These glances become more frequent, and suddenly the eyes of both boys fill with tears. Then they look up no more, but keep their eyes obstinately lowered.

It seems that when the peasant woman entered some one else — some one who was invisible and imperceptible to all save the boys — came into the coupé. The boys fancied that she came and sat down between them and took their hands in hers, as she had done late last night, when it was settled that they must leave her; and she was talking to them now as she did then. "You must promise me that you will not be angry with father for my sake. Father has never been able to forgive me for preventing him from going abroad. He thinks it is my fault that he has never amounted to anything and that he drinks. He can never punish me enough. But you must n't be angry at him on that account. Now, when you are to live with father, you must promise me that you will be kind to him. You must n't quarrel with him and you are to look after his needs as well as you can. This you must promise me, otherwise I don't know how I can ever let you go." And the boys promised. " You must n't run away from father, promise me that!" mother had said. That they had also promised.

The boys are as good as their word, and the instant they happen to think that they had given mother these promises, they abandon all thought of flight. Father sleeps all the while and they remain patiently in their places. Then they resume their reading with redoubled zeal, and their friend, the good Jules Verne, soon takes them away from many heavy sorrows to Africa's happy wonder world.

Far out on the south side of the city, father has rented two rooms and a kitchen on the ground floor, with an entrance from the court and an outlook over a narrow yard. The apartment has long been in use; it has gone from family to family, without ever having been renovated. The wall paper is full of tears and spots; the ceilings are sooty; a couple of window-panes are cracked, and the kitchen floor is so worn that it is full of ruts. Expressmen have brought the furniture cases from the railway station and have left them there, helter skelter. Father and the boys are now unpacking. Father stands with axe raised to hack open a box. The boys are taking out glass and porcelain ware from another box, and are arranging them in a wall cupboard. They are handy and work eagerly, but the father never stops cautioning them to be careful, and forbids their carrying more than one glass or plate at a time. Meanwhile it goes slowly with father's own work. His hands are fumbly and powerless, and he works himself into a sweat without getting the lock off the box. He lays down the axe, walks around the box, and wonders if it 's the bottom that is uppermost. Then one of the boys takes hold of the axe and begins to bend the lock, but father pushes him aside. " That lock is nailed down too hard. Surely you don't imagine that you can force the lock when father could n't do it? Only a regular workman can open that box," says father, putting on his hat and coat to go and fetch the janitor.

Father is hardly outside the door when an idea strikes him. Instantly he understands why he has no strength in his hands. It is still quite early in the morning and he has not consumed

anything which could set the blood in motion.
If he were to step into a café and have a cognac,
he would get back his strength and could manage without help. This is better than calling
the janitor.

Then father goes into the street to try and
hunt up a café. When he returns to the little
apartment on the court, it is eight o'clock in the
evening.

In father's youth, when he attended the Academy, he had lived at the south end of the city.
He was then a member of a double quartette,
mostly made up of choristers and petty trades-
men, who used to meet in a cellar near Mose-
backe. Father had taken a notion to go and see
if the little cellar was still there. It was, in fact,
and father had the luck to run across a pair of
old comrades who were seated there having
their breakfast. They had received him with
the greatest delight, had invited him to breakfast, and had celebrated his advent in Stockholm
in the friendliest way possible. When the
breakfast was over, finally, father wanted to go
home and unpack his furniture, but his friends
persuaded him to remain and take dinner with
them. This function was so long drawn out that
he had n't been able to go home until around
eight o'clock. And it had cost him more than a

slight effort to tear himself away from the lively place that early.

When father comes home, the boys are in the dark, for they have no matches. Father has a match in his pocket, and when he has lighted a little stump of a candle, which luckily had come along with their furnishings, he sees that the boys are hot and dusty, but well and happy and apparently very well pleased with their day.

In the rooms the furniture is arranged alongside the walls, the boxes have been removed and straw and papers have been swept away. Hugo is just turning down the boys' beds in the outer room. The inner room is to be father's bedroom, and there stands his bed, turned down with as great care as he could possibly wish.

Now a sudden revulsion of feeling possesses him. When he came home, he was displeased with himself because he had gone away from his work and had left the boys without food; but now, when he sees that they are in good spirits and not in any distress, he regrets that, for their sakes, he should have left his friends; and he becomes irritable and quarrelsome.

He sees, no doubt, that the boys are proud of all the work they have accomplished and expect him to praise them; but this he is not at all inclined to do. Instead, he asks who has been here and helped them, and begs them to remember that here in Stockholm one gets nothing without money, and that the janitor must be paid for all he does. The boys answer that they have had no assistance and have got on by themselves. But father continues to grumble. It was wrong of them to open the big box. They might have hurt themselves on it. Had he not forbidden them to open it? Now they would have to obey him. He is the one who must answer for their welfare.

He takes the candle, goes out into the kitchen, and peeps into the cupboards. The scanty supply of glass and porcelain is arranged on the shelves in an orderly manner. He scrutinizes everything very carefully to find an excuse for further complaint.

All of a sudden he catches sight of some leavings from the boys' supper, and begins immediately to grumble because they have had chicken. Where did they get it from? Do they think of living like princes? Is it his money they are throwing away on chicken? Then he remembers that he had not left them any money. He wonders if they have stolen the chicken and becomes perturbed. He preaches and admonishes, scolds and fusses, but now he gets no response from the boys. They do not bother themselves about telling him where they got the chicken, but let him go on. He makes long speeches and exhausts his forces. Finally he begs and implores.

"I beseech you to tell me the truth. I will forgive you, no matter what you have done, if you will only tell me the truth!"

Now the boys can hold in no longer. Father hears a spluttering sound. They throw off the quilts and sit up, and he notices that they are purple in the face from suppressed laughter. And as they can laugh now without restraint, Lennart says between the paroxysms, "Mother put a chicken in the food sack which she gave us when we left home."

Father draws himself up, looks at the boys, wants to speak, but finds no suitable words. He becomes even more majestic in his bearing, looks with withering scorn at them, and goes to his room without further parley.

It has dawned upon father how handy the boys are, and he makes use of this fact to escape hiring servants. Mornings he sends Lennart into the kitchen to make coffee and lets Hugo lay the breakfast-table and fetch bread from the baker's. After breakfast he sits down on a chair and watches how the boys make up the beds, sweep the floors, and build a fire in the grate. He gives endless orders and sends them from one task to another, only to show his authority. When the morning chores are over, he goes out and remains away all the forenoon. The dinner he lets them fetch from a cooking-school in the neighborhood. After dinner he leaves the boys for the evening, and exacts nothing more of them than that his bed shall be turned down when he comes home.

The boys are practically alone almost the entire day and can busy themselves in any way they choose.

One of their most important tasks is to write to their mother. They get letters from her every day, and she sends them paper and postage, so that they can answer her. Mother's letters are mostly admonitions that they shall be good to their father. She writes constantly of how lovable father was when she first knew him, of how industrious and thrifty he was at the beginning of his career. They must be tender and kind to him. They must never forget how unhappy he is. "If you are very good to father, perhaps he may feel sorry for you and let you come home to me."

Mother tells them that she has called to see

the dean and the burgomaster to ask if it were
not possible to get back the boys. Both of them
had replied that there was no help for her. The
boys would have to stay with their father.
Mother wants to move to Stockholm that she
may see her boys once in a while, at least, but
every one advises her to have patience and
abide her time. They think father will soon
tire of the boys and send them home. Mother
does n't quite know what she should do. On
the one hand she thinks it dreadful that the
boys are living in Stockholm with no one to
look after them, and on the other hand she
knows that if she were to leave her home and
her work, she could not take them and support
them, even if they were freed. But for Christmas, at all events, mother is coming to Stockholm to look after them.

The boys write and tell her what they do all
day, hour by hour. They let mother know that
they cook for father and make his bed. She ap-
prehends that they are trying to be kind to him
for her sake, but she probably perceives that
they like him no better now than formerly.

Her little boys appear to be always alone.
They live in a large city, where there are lots of
people, but no one asks after them. And perhaps it is better thus. Who can tell what

might happen to them were they to make any acquaintances?

They always beg of her not to be uneasy about them. They tell how they darn their stockings and sew on their buttons. They also intimate that Lennart has made great headway with his invention and say that when this is finished all will be well.

Mother lives in a state of continual fear. Night and day her thoughts are with her boys. Night and day she prays God to watch over her little sons, who live alone in a great city, with no one to shield them from the temptations of the destroyer, and to keep their young hearts from the desire for evil.

Father and the boys are sitting one morning at the Opera. One of father's old comrades, who is with the Royal Orchestra, has invited him to be present at a symphony rehearsal, and father has taken the boys along. When the orchestra strikes up and the auditorium is filled with tone, father is so affected that he can't control himself, and begins to weep. He sobs and blows his nose and moans aloud, time and again. He puts no restraint upon his feelings, but makes such a noise that the musicians are disturbed. A guard comes along and beckons him away, and

father takes the boys by the hand and slinks out
without a word of protest. All the way home
his tears continue to flow.

Father is walking on, with a boy on each
side, and he has kept their hands in his all the
while. Suddenly the boys start crying. They
understand now for the first time how much
father has loved his art. It was painful for him
to sit there, besotten and broken, and listen to
others playing. They feel sorry for him who
had never become what he might have been. It
was with father as it might be with Lennart
were he never to finish his flying-machine, or
with Hugo if he were not to make any voyages
of discovery. Think if they should one day sit
like old good-for-nothings and see fine airships
sailing over their heads which they had not invented and were not allowed to pilot!

The boys were sitting one morning on opposite
sides of the writing-table. Father had taken a
music roll under his arm and gone out. He had
mumbled something about giving a music lesson, but the boys had not for a moment been
tempted into believing this true.

Father is in an ugly mood as he walks up the
street. He noticed the look the boys exchanged
when he said that he was going to a music les-

son. "They are setting themselves up as judges of their father," he thinks. "I am too indulgent toward them. I should have given them each a sound box on the ear. It 's their mother, I dare say, who is setting them against me. Suppose I were to keep an eye on the fine gentlemen?" he continues. "It would do no harm to find out how they attend to their lessons."

He turns back, walks quietly across the court, opens the door very softly, and stands in the boys' room without either of them having heard him coming. The boys jump up, red in the face, and Lennart quickly snatches a bundle of papers which he throws into the table drawer.

When the boys had been in Stockholm a day or two, they had asked which school they were to attend, and the father had replied that their school-going days were over now. He would try and procure a private tutor who would teach them. This proposition he had never carried into effect, nor had the boys said anything more about going to school. But in less than a week a school chart was discovered hanging on the wall in the boys' room. The school books had been brought forth, and every morning they sat on opposite sides of an old writing-table and studied their lessons aloud. It was evident that they had received letters from their mother counselling them to try and study, so as not to forget entirely what they had learned.

Now, as father unexpectedly comes into the room, he goes up to the chart first and studies it. He takes out his watch and compares. "Wednesday, between ten and eleven, Geography." Then he comes up to the table. "Should n't you have geography at this hour?"

"Yes," the boys reply, growing flame-red in the face.

"Have you the geography and the map?"

The boys glance over at the book shelf and look confused. "We have n't begun yet," says Lennart.

"Indeed!" says father. "You must have been up to something else." He straightens up, thoroughly pleased with himself. He has an advantage, which he does n't care to let go until he has browbeaten them very effectually.

Both boys are silent. Ever since the day they accompanied father to the Opera, they have felt sympathy for him, and it has not been such an effort for them to be kind to him as it was before. But, naturally, they have n't for a moment thought of taking father into their confidence. He has not risen in their estimation although they are sorry for him.

"Were you writing letters?" father asks in his severest tone.

"No," say both boys at the same time.

"What were you doing?"

"Oh, just talking."

"That is n't true. I saw that Lennart hid something in the drawer of the table."

Now both boys are mum again.

"Take it out!" shouts the father, purple with rage. He thinks the sons have written to his wife, and, since they don't care to show the letter, of course there is something mean about him in it.

The boys do not stir, and father raises his hand to strike Lennart, who is sitting before the table drawer.

"Don't touch him!" cries Hugo. "We were only talking over something which Lennart has invented."

Hugo pushes Lennart aside, opens the drawer, and pulls out the paper, which is scrawled full of airships of the most extraordinary shapes. "Last night Lennart thought out a new kind of sail for his airship. It was of this we were speaking."

Father would n't believe him. He bends over, searches in the drawer, but finds only sheets of paper covered with drawings of balloons, parachutes, flying-machines, and everything else appertaining to air-sailing.

To the great surprise of the boys, father does

not cast this aside at once, nor does he laugh at
their attempts, but examines closely sheet after
sheet. As a matter of fact, father, too, has a
little leaning toward mechanics, and was interested in things of this sort in days gone by, when
his brain was still good for something. Soon he
begins to ask questions as to the meaning of one
thing and another, and inasmuch as his words
betray that he is deeply interested and understands what he sees, Lennart fights his bashful-
ness, and answers him, hesitatingly at first and
then more willingly.

Soon father and boys are absorbed in a profound discussion about airships and air-sailing.
After they are fairly well started, the boys
chatter unreservedly and give father a share in
their plans and dreams of greatness. And while
the father comprehends, of course, that the boys
cannot fly very far with the airship which they
have constructed, he is very much impressed.
His little sons talk of aluminum motors, aero-
planes, and balancers, as though they were the
simplest things in the world. He had thought
them regular blockheads because they did n't
get on very fast at school. Now, all at once, he
believes they are a pair of little scientists.

The high-soaring thoughts and aspirations
father understands better than anything else;

he cognizes them. He himself has dreamed in the same way, and he has no desire to laugh at such dreams.

Father does n't go out again that morning, but sits and chats with the boys until it is time to fetch the food for dinner and set the table. And at that meal father and the boys are real good friends, to their great and mutual astonishment.

The hour is eleven at night, and father is staggering up the street. The little boys are walking on either side of him, and he holds their hands tightly clasped in his all the while.

They have sought him out in one of his haunts, where they have stationed themselves just inside the door. Father sits by himself at a table with a big brown toddy in front of him, and listens to a ladies' orchestra which is playing at the other end of the hall. After a moment's hesitancy he rises reluctantly and goes over to the boys. "What is it?" he asks. "Why do you come here?"

"Father was to come home," they say. "This is the fifth of December. Father promised—"

Then he remembers that Lennart had confided to him that it was Hugo's birthday and that he had promised him to come home early. But this he had entirely forgotten. Hugo was probably expecting a birthday present from him, but he had not remembered to get him one.

At any rate, he has gone with the boys and is walking along, displeased with them and with himself. When he comes home, the birthday table is laid. The boys had wished to give a little party. Lennart had creamed some pancakes, which are now a few hours old and look like pieces of leather. They had received a little money from their mother, and with this they had bought nuts, raisins, and a bottle of soda-water.

This fine feast they did not care to enjoy all by themselves, and they had been sitting and waiting for father to come home and share it with them. Now, since they and father have become friends, they cannot celebrate such a big event without him. Father understands it all, and the thought of being missed flatters him and puts him in a fairly good humor. Half full as he is, he plumps himself down at the table. Just as he is about to take his place he stumbles, clutches at the table-cloth, falls, and draws down on the floor everything on the table. As he raises himself, he sees how the soda flows out over the floor and pickles and pancakes are strewn about among bits of porcelain and broken glass.

Father glances at the boys' long faces, rips out an oath, and makes a rush for the door, and he does n't come back home until on towards morning.

One morning in February, the boys are coming up the street with their skates dangling from their shoulders. They are not quite like themselves. They have grown thin and pale and look untidy and uncared for. Their hair is uncut; they are not well washed and they have holes in both stockings and shoes. When they address each other, they use a lot of street-boy expressions, and one and another oath escapes from their lips.

A change has taken place in the boys. It had its beginning on the evening when their father forgot to come home to help celebrate Hugo's birthday. It was as if until that time they had been kept up by the hope that soon their father would be a changed man.

At first they had counted on his tiring of them and sending them home. Later, they had fancied that he would become fond of them and give up drinking for their sakes, and they had even imagined that mother and he might become reconciled and that all of them would be happy. But it dawned upon them that night that father was impossible. He could love nothing but drink. Even if he were kind to them for a little while, he did n't really care for them.

A heavy hopelessness fell upon the boys; nothing would ever be changed for them. They should never get away from father. They felt as though they were doomed to sit shut in a dark prison all their lives. Not even their great plans for the future could comfort them. In the way that they were bound down, these plans could never be carried out. Only think, they were not learning anything! They knew enough of the histories of great men to know that he who wants to accomplish anything noteworthy must first of all have knowledge.

Still the hardest blow was that mother did not come to them at Christmas. In the beginning of December she had fallen down stairs and broken her leg, and was forced to lie in a hospital during the Christmas holidays, therefore she could not come to Stockholm. Now that mother was up, her school had begun again. Apart from this, she had no money with which to travel. The little that she had saved was spent while she lay ill.

The boys felt themselves deserted by the whole world. It was obvious that it never would be any better for them, no matter how good they were! So, gradually, they ceased to exert themselves with the sort of things that were tiresome. They might just as well do that which amused them.

The boys began to shirk their morning studies. No one heard their lessons, so what was the use of their studying? There had been good skating for a couple of days and they might as well play truant all day. On the ice there were always throngs of boys, and they had made the acquaintance of a number who also preferred skating to being shut in the house with their books.

It has turned out to be such a fine day that it is impossible to think of staying indoors. The weather is so clear and sunny that the school children have been granted skating leave. The whole street is filled with children, who have been home to get their skates and are now hurrying down to the ice.

The boys, as they move among the other children, appear solemn and low-spirited. Not a smile lights up their faces. Their misfortune is so heavy that they cannot forget it for a second.

When they come down on the ice, it is full of life and movement. All along the edges it is bordered with a tight mass of people; farther out, the skaters circle around one another, like gnats, and still farther out, solitary black specks that float along at lightning speed are seen.

The boys buckle on their skates and join the other skaters. They skate very well, and as they glide out on the ice, full speed, they get color in their cheeks and their eyes sparkle, but not for a moment do they appear happy, like other children.

All of a sudden, as they are making a turn toward land, they catch sight of something very pretty. A big balloon comes from the direction of Stockholm and is sailing out toward Salt Lake. It is striped in reds and yellows, and when the sun strikes it it glitters like a ball of fire. The basket is decorated with many-hued flags, and as the balloon does not fly very high the bright color-play can be seen quite plainly.

When the boys spy the balloon, they send up a shriek of delight. It is the first time in their lives that they have seen a big balloon sailing through the air. All the dreams and plans which have been their consolation and joy during the many trying days come back to them when they see it. They stand still that they may observe how the ropes and lines are fastened; and they take note of the anchor and the sand bags on the edge of the car.

The balloon moves with good speed over the ice-bound fiord. All the skaters, big and little, dart around one another, laughing and hooting at it when it first comes into sight, and then they bound after it. They follow it out to sea, in a long swaying line, like a drag line. The air-sailors amuse themselves by scattering handfuls of paper strips in a variety of colors, which come circling down slowly through the blue air.

The boys are foremost in the long line that is chasing after the balloon. They hurry forward, with heads thrown back, and gaze steadily turned upward. Their eyes dance with delight for the first time since they parted from their mother. They are beside themselves with excitement over the airship and think of nothing else than to follow it as long as possible.

But the balloon moves ahead rapidly, and one has to be a good skater not to be left behind. The crowd chasing after it thins down, but in the lead of those who keep up the pursuit the two little boys are seen. Afterwards people said there was something strange about them. They neither laughed nor shouted, but on their upturned faces there was a look of transport — as though they had seen a heavenly vision.

The balloon also affects the boys like a celestial guide, who has come to lead them back to the right path and teach them how to go forward with renewed courage. When the boys see it, their hearts bound with longing to begin work again on the great invention. Once more they feel confident and happy. If only they are patient, they'll probably work their way toward success. A day will surely come when they can step into their own airship and soar aloft in space. Some day *they* will be the ones who travel up there, far above the people, and *their* airship will be more perfect than the one they now see. Theirs shall be an airship that can be steered and turned, lowered and raised, sail against wind and without wind. It shall carry them by day and by night, wherever they may wish to travel. They shall descend to the highest mountain peaks, travel over the dreariest deserts, and explore the most inaccessible regions. They shall behold all the glories of the world.

"It is n't worth while to lose heart, Hugo," says Lennart. "We'll have a fine time if we can only finish it!"

Father and his ill-luck are things which do not concern them any more. One who has something as great to strive for as they have cannot let himself be hindered by anything so pitiable!

The balloon gains in speed the farther out it

comes. The skaters have ceased following it. The only ones who continue the chase are the two little boys. They move ahead as swiftly and lightly as if their feet had taken on wings.

Suddenly the people who stand on the shore and can look far out across the fiord send up a great cry of horror and fear. They see that the balloon, pursued all the while by the two children, sails away toward the fairway, where there is open sea. "Open sea! It is open sea out there!" the people shout.

The skaters down on the ice hear the shouts and turn their eyes toward the mouth of the fiord. They see how a strip of water shimmers in the sunlight yonder. They see, also, that two little boys are skating toward this strip, which they do not notice because their eyes are fixed on the balloon; and not for a second do they turn them toward earth.

The people are calling out with all their might and stamping on the ice. Fast runners are hurrying on to stop them; but the little ones mark nothing of all this, where they are chasing after the airship. They do not know that they alone are following it. They hear no cries back of them. They do not hear the splash and roar of the water ahead of them. They see only the balloon, which as it were carries them with it..

Lennart already feels his own airship rising under him, and Hugo soars away over the North Pole.

The people on the ice and on the shore see how rapidly they are nearing the open sea. For a second or two they are in such breathless suspense that they can neither move nor cry out. It seems as if the two children are under a magic spell — in their chase after a shining heavenly vision.

The air-sailors up in the balloon have also caught a glimpse of the little boys. They see that they are in danger and scream at them and make warning gestures; but the boys do not understand them. When they notice that the air-sailors are making signs at them, they think they want to take them up into the car. They stretch their arms toward them, overjoyed in the hope of accompanying them through the bright upper regions.

At this moment the boys have reached the sailing channel, and, with arms uplifted, they skate down into the water and disappear without a cry for help. The skaters, who have tried to reach them in time, are standing a couple of seconds later on the edge of the ice, but the current has carried their bodies under the ice, and no helping hand can reach them.

The Wedding March

The Wedding March

Now I 'm going to tell a pretty story.

A good many years ago there was to be a very big wedding at Svartsjö parish in Vermland.

First, there was to be a church ceremony and after that three days of feasting and merrymaking, and every day while the festivities lasted there was to be dancing from early morning till far into the night.

Since there was to be so much dancing, it was of very great importance to get a good fiddler, and Juryman Nils Olafsson, who was managing the wedding, worried almost more over this than over anything else.

The fiddler they had at Svartsjö he did not care to engage. His name was Jan Öster. The Juryman knew, to be sure, that he had quite a big name; but he was so poor that sometimes he would appear at a wedding in a frayed jacket and without shoes to his feet. The Juryman did n't wish to see such a ragtag at the head of the bridal ·procession, so he decided to send a messenger to a musician in Jösse parish, who was

commonly called Fiddler Mårten, and ask him
if he would n't come and play at the wedding.

Fiddler Mårten did n't consider the proposition for a second, but promptly replied that he
did not want to play at Svartsjö, because in
that parish lived a musician who was more
skilled than all others in Vermland. While
they had him, there was no need for them to
call another.

When Nils Olafsson received this answer, he
took a few days to think it over, and then he
sent word to a fiddler in Big Kil parish, named
Olle in Säby, to ask him if he would n't come
and play at his daughter's wedding.

Olle in Säby answered in the same way as
Fiddler Mårten. He sent his compliments to
Nils Olafsson, and said that so long as there
was such a capable musician as Jan Öster to be
had in Svartsjö, he did n't want to go there to
play.

Nils Olafsson did n't like it that the musicians
tried in this way to force upon him the very
one he did not want. Now he considered that
it was a point of honor with him to get another
fiddler than Jan Öster.

A few days after he had the answer from Olle
in Säby, he sent his servant to fiddler Lars Larsson, who lived at the game lodge in Ullerud

parish. Lars Larsson was a well-to-do man who owned a fine farm. He was sensible and considerate and no hotspur, like the other musicians. But Lars Larsson, like the others, at once thought of Jan Öster, and asked how it happened that he was not to play at the wedding.

Nils Olafsson's servant thought it best to say to him that, since Jan Öster lived at Svartsjö, they could hear him play at any time. As Nils Olafsson was making ready to give a grand wedding, he wished to treat his guests to something a little better and more select.

"I doubt if you can get any one better," said Lars Larsson.

"Now you must be thinking of answering in the same way as fiddler Mårten and Olle in Säby did," said the servant. Then he told him how he had fared with them.

Lars Larsson paid close attention to the servant's story, and then he sat quietly for a long while and pondered. Finally he answered in the affirmative: "Tell your master that I thank him for his invitation and will come."

The following Sunday Lars Larsson journeyed down to Svartsjö. He drove up to the church knoll just as the wedding guests were forming into line to march to the church. He came driving in his own chaise and with a good horse and dressed in black broadcloth. He took out his fiddle from a highly polished box. Nils Olafsson received him effusively, thinking that here was a fiddler of whom he might be proud.

Immediately after Lars Larsson's arrival, Jan Öster, too, came marching up to the church, with his fiddle under his arm. He walked straight up to the crowd around the bride, exactly as if he were asked to come and play at the wedding.

Jan Öster had come in the old gray homespun jacket which they had seen him wearing for ages. But, as this was to be such a grand wedding, his wife had made an attempt at mending the holes at the elbow by sewing big green patches over them. Jan Öster was a tall handsome man, and would have made a fine appearance at the head of the bridal procession, had he not been so shabbily dressed, and had his face not been so lined and seamed by worries and the hard struggle with misfortune.

When Lars Larsson saw Jan Öster coming, he seemed a bit displeased. "So you have called Jan Öster, too," he said under his breath to the Juryman Nils Olafsson, "but at a grand wedding there's no harm in having two fiddlers."

"I did not invite him, that's certain!" protested Nils Olafsson. "I can't comprehend why

he has come. Just wait, and I'll let him know
that he has no business here!"

"Then some practical joker must have bidden
him," said Lars Larsson. "But if you care to
be guided by my counsel, appear as if nothing
were wrong and go over and bid him welcome. I
have heard said that he is a quick-tempered
man, and who knows but he may begin to
quarrel and fight if you were to tell him that
he was not invited?"

This the Juryman knew, too! It was no time
to begin fussing when the bridal procession was
forming on the church grounds; so he walked
up to Jan Öster and bade him be welcome.
Thereupon the two fiddlers took their places at
the head of the procession. The bridal pair
walked under a canopy, the bridesmaids and the
groomsmen marched in pairs, and after them
came the parents and relatives; so the procession was both imposing and long.

When everything was in readiness, a groomsman stepped up to the musicians and asked
them to play the Wedding March. Both musicians swung their fiddles up to their chins, but
beyond that they did not get. And thus they
stood! It was an old custom in Svartsjö for
the best fiddler to strike up the Wedding March
and to lead the music.

The groomsman looked at Lars Larsson, as though he were waiting for him to start; but Lars Larsson looked at Jan Öster and said, "It is you, Jan Öster, who must begin."

It did not seem possible to Jan Öster that the other fiddler, who was as finely dressed as any gentleman, should not be better than himself, who had come in his old homespun jacket straight from the wretched hovel where there were only poverty and distress. "No, indeed!" said he. "No, indeed!"

He saw that the bridegroom put forth his hand and touched Lars Larsson. "Larsson shall begin," said he.

When Jan Öster heard the bridegroom say this, he promptly lowered his fiddle and stepped aside.

Lars Larsson, on the other hand, did not move from the spot, but remained standing in his place, confident and pleased with himself. Nor did he raise the bow. "It is Jan Öster who shall begin," he repeated stubbornly and resistingly, as one who is used to having his own way.

There was some commotion among the crowds over the cause of the delay. The bride's father came forward and begged Lars Larsson to begin. The sexton stepped to the door of the church and beckoned to them to hurry along. The parson stood waiting at the altar.

"You can ask Jan Öster to begin, then," said Lars Larsson. "We musicians consider him to be the best among us."

"That may be so," said a peasant, "but we peasants consider you the best one."

Then the other peasants also gathered around them. "Well, begin, why don't you?" they said. "The parson is waiting. We'll become a laughing-stock to the church people."

Lars Larsson stood there quite as stubborn and determined as before. "I can't see why the people in this parish are so opposed to having their own fiddler placed in the lead."

Nils Olafsson was perfectly furious because they wished in this way to force Jan Öster upon him. He came close up to Lars Larsson and whispered: "I comprehend that it is you who have called hither Jan Öster, and that you have arranged this to do him honor. But be quick, now, and play up, or I'll drive that ragamuffin from the church grounds in disgrace and by force!"

Lars Larsson looked him square in the face and nodded to him without displaying any irritation. "Yes, you are right in saying that we must have an end of this," said he.

He beckoned to Jan Öster to return to his place. Then he himself walked forward a step or two, and turned around that all might see him. Then he flung the bow far from him, pulled out his case-knife, and cut all four violin strings, which snapped with a sharp twang. "It shall not be said of me that I count myself better than Jan Öster!" said he.

It appears that for three years Jan Öster had been musing on an air which he could n't get out over the strings because at home he was bound down by dull, gray cares and worries, and nothing ever happened to him, either great or small, to lift him above the daily grind. But when he heard Lars Larsson's strings snap, he threw back his head and filled his lungs. His features were rapt, as though he were listening to something far away; and then he began to play. And the air which he had been musing over for three years became all at once clear to him, and as the tones of it vibrated he walked with proud step down to the church.

The bridal procession had never before heard an air like that! It carried them along with such speed that not even Nils Olafsson could think of staying back. And every one was so pleased both with Jan Öster and with Lars Larsson that the entire following entered the church, their eyes brimming with tears of joy.

The Musician

The Musician

No one in Ullerud could say anything of fiddler
Lars Larsson but that he was both meek and
modest in his later years. But he had not always
been thus, it seems. In his youth he had been
so overbearing and boastful that people were
in despair about him. It is said that he was
changed and made over in a single night, and
this is the way it happened.

Lars Larsson went out for a stroll late one
Saturday night, with his fiddle under his arm.
He was excessively gay and jovial, for he had
just come from a party where his playing had
tempted both young and old to dance. He
walked along, thinking that while his bow was
in motion no one had been able to sit still.
There had been such a whirl in the cabin that
once or twice he fancied the chairs and tables
were dancing too! "I verily believe they have
never before had a musician like me in these
parts," he remarked to himself. "But I had a
mighty rough time of it before I became such a
clever chap!" he continued. "When I was a

child, it was no fun for me when my parents put me to tending cows and sheep and when I forgot everything else to sit and twang my fiddle. And just fancy! they would n't so much as give me a real violin. I had nothing to play on but an old wooden box over which I had stretched some strings. In the daytime, when I could be alone in the woods, I fared rather well; but it was none too cheerful to come home in the evening when the cattle had strayed from me! Then I heard often enough, from both father and mother, that I was a good-for-nothing and never would amount to anything."

In that part of the forest where Lars Larsson was strolling a little river was trying to find its way. The ground was stony and hilly, and the stream had great difficulty in getting ahead, winding this way and that way, rolling over little falls and rapids — and yet it appeared to get nowhere. The path where the fiddler walked, on the other hand, tried to go as straight ahead as possible. Therefore it was continually meeting the sinuous stream, and each time it would dart across it by using a little bridge. The musician also had to cross the stream repeatedly, and he was glad of it. He thought it was as though he had found company in the forest.

Where he was tramping it was light summer-
night. The sun had not yet come up, but its
being away made no difference, for it was as
light as day all the same.

Still the light was not quite what it is in the
daytime. Everything had a different color.
The sky was perfectly white, the trees and the
growths on the ground were grayish, but everything was as distinctly visible as in the daytime,
and when Lars Larsson paused on any of the
numerous bridges and looked down into the
stream, he could distinguish every ripple on the
water.

"When I see a stream like this in the wilderness," he thought, "I am reminded of my own
life. As persistent as this stream have I been in
forcing my way past all that has obstructed my
path. Father has been my rock ahead, and
mother tried to hold me back and bury me
between moss-tufts, but I stole past both of
them and got out in the world. Hay-ho, hi, hi!
I think mother is still sitting at home and weeping for me. But what do I care! She might
have known that I should amount to something
some day, instead of trying to oppose me!"

Impatiently he tore some leaves from a branch
and threw them into the river.

"Look! thus have I torn myself loose from

everything at home," he said, as he watched the leaves borne away by the water. "I am just wondering if mother knows that I'm the best musician in Vermland?" he remarked as he went farther.

He walked on rapidly until he came across the stream again. Then he stopped and looked into the water.

Here the river went along in a struggling rapid, creating a terrible racket. As it was night, one heard from the stream sounds quite different from those of the daytime, and the musician was perfectly astonished when he stood still and listened. There was no bird song in the trees and no music in the pines and no rustling in the leaves. No wagon wheels creaked in the road and no cow-bells tinkled in the wood. One heard only the rapid; but because all the other things were hushed, it could be heard so much better than during the day. It sounded as though everything thinkable and unthinkable was rioting and clamoring in the depths of the stream. First, it sounded as if some one were sitting down there and grinding grain between stones, and then it sounded as though goblets were clinking in a drinking-bout; and again there was a murmuring, as when the congregation had left the church and were standing on the church knoll after the service, talking earnestly together.

"I suppose this, too, is a kind of music," thought the fiddler, "although I can't find anything much in it! I think the air that I composed the other day was much more worth listening to."

But the longer Lars Larsson listened to the music of the rapid, the better he thought it sounded.

"I believe you are improving," he said to the rapid. "It must have dawned upon you that the best musician in Vermland is listening to you!"

The instant he had made this remark, he fancied he heard a couple of clear metallic sounds, as when some one picks a violin string to hear if it is in tune.

"But see, hark! The Water-Sprite himself has arrived. I can hear how he begins to thrum on the violin. Let us hear now if you can play better than I!" said Lars Larsson, laughing. "But I can't stand here all night waiting for you to begin," he called to the water. "Now I must be going; but I promise you that I will also stop at the next bridge and listen, to hear if you can cope with me."

He went farther and, as the stream in its

winding course ran into the wood, he began
thinking once more of his home.

"I wonder how the little brooklet that runs
by our house is getting on? I should like to see
it again. I ought to go home once in a while,
to see if mother is suffering want and hardship
since father's death. But busy as I am, it is
almost impossible. As busy as I am just now,
I say, I can't look after anything but the fiddle.
There is hardly an evening in the week that I
am at liberty."

In a little while he met the stream again, and
his thoughts were turned to something else.
At this crossing the river did not come rushing
on in a noisy rapid, but glided ahead rather
quietly. It lay perfectly black and shiny under
the night-gray forest trees, and carried with it
one and another patch of snow-white scum
from the rapids above.

When the musician came down upon the
bridge and heard no sound from the stream
but a soft swish now and then, he began to
laugh.

"I might have known that the Water-Sprite
would n't care to come to the meeting," he
shouted. "To be sure, I have always heard
that he is considered an excellent performer, but
one who lies still forever in a brook and never

hears anything new can't know very much!
He perceives, no doubt, that here stands one
who knows more about music than he, therefore he does n't care to let me hear him."

Then he went farther and lost sight of the
river again. He came into a part of the forest
which he had always thought dismal and
bleak to wander through. There the ground was
covered with big stone heaps, and gnarled pine
stumps lay uprooted among them. If there
was anything magical or fearsome in the forest,
one would naturally think that it concealed
itself here.

When the musician came in among the wild
stone blocks, a shudder passed through him, and
he began to wonder if it had not been unwise of
him to boast in the presence of the Water-
Sprite. He fancied the large pine roots began
to gesticulate, as if they were threatening him.
"Beware, you who think yourself cleverer than
the Water-Sprite!" it seemed as if they wanted
to say.

Lars Larsson felt how his heart contracted
with dread. A heavy weight bore down upon
his chest, so that he could scarcely breathe, and
his hands became ice-cold. Then he stopped in
the middle of the wood and tried to talk sense
to himself.

"Why, there's no musician in the waterfall!" said he. "Such things are only superstition and nonsense! It 's of no consequence what I have said or have n't said to him."

As he spoke, he looked around him, as if for some confirmation of the truth of what he said. Had it been daytime, every tiny leaf would have winked at him that there was nothing dangerous in the wood; but now, at night, the leaves on the trees were closed and silent and looked as though they were hiding all sorts of dangerous secrets.

Lars Larsson grew more and more alarmed. That which caused him the greatest fear was having to cross the stream once more before it and the road parted company and went in different directions. He wondered what the Water-Sprite would do to him when he walked across the last bridge — if he might perhaps stretch a big black hand out of the water and drag him down into the depths.

He had worked himself into such a state of fright that he thought of turning back. But then he would meet the stream again. And if he were to turn out of the road and go into the wood, he would also meet it, the way it kept bending and winding itself!

He felt so nervous that he did n't know

what to do. He was snared and captured and
bound by that stream, and saw no possibility of
escape.

Finally he saw before him the last bridge
crossing. Directly opposite him, on the other
side of the stream, stood an old mill, which must
have been abandoned these many years. The
big mill-wheel hung motionless over the water.
The sluice-gate lay mouldering on the land; the
mill-race was moss-grown, and its sides were
lined with common fern and beard-moss.

"If all had been as formerly and there were
people here," thought the musician, "I should
be safe now from all danger."

But, at all events, he felt reassured in seeing
a building constructed by human hands, and, as
he crossed the stream, he was scarcely frightened
at all. Nor did anything dreadful happen to
him. The Water-Sprite seemed to have no
quarrel with him. He was simply amazed to
think he had worked himself into a panic over
nothing whatever.

He felt very happy and' secure, and became
even happier when the mill door opened and a
young girl came out to him. She looked like
an ordinary peasant girl. She had a cotton
kerchief on her head and wore a short skirt and
full jacket, but her feet were bare.

She walked up to the musician and said to him without further ceremony, "If you will play for me, I 'll dance for you."

"Why, certainly," said the fiddler, who was in fine spirits now that he was rid of his fear. "That I can do, of course. I have never in my life refused to play for a pretty girl who wants to dance."

He took his place on a stone near the edge of the mill-pond, raised the violin to his chin, and began to play.

The girl took a few steps in rhythm with the music; then she stopped. "What kind of a polka are you playing?" said she. "There is no vim in it."

The fiddler changed his tune; he tried one with more life in it.

The girl was just as dissatisfied. "I can't dance to such a draggy polka," said she.

Then Lars Larsson struck up the wildest air he knew. "If you are not satisfied with this one," he said, "you will have to call hither a better musician than I am."

The instant he said this, he felt that a hand caught his arm at the elbow and began to guide the bow and increase the tempo. Then from the violin there poured forth a strain the like of which he had never before heard. It moved in such a quick tempo he thought that a rolling wheel could n't have kept up with it.

"Now, that 's what I call a polka!" said the girl, and began to swing round.

But the musician did not glance at her. He was so astonished at the air he was playing that he stood with closed eyes, to hear better. When he opened them after a moment, the girl was gone. But he did not wonder much at this. He continued to play on, long and well, only because he had never before heard such violin playing.

"It must be time now to finish with this," he thought finally, and wanted to lay down the bow. But the bow kept up its motion; he could n't make it stop. It travelled back and forth over the strings and jerked the hand and arm with it; and the hand that held the neck of the violin and fingered the strings could not free itself, either.

The cold sweat stood out on Lars Larsson's brow, and he was frightened now in earnest.

"How will this end? Shall I sit here and play till doomsday?" he asked himself in despair.

The bow ran on and on, and magically called forth one tune after another. Always it was something new, and it was so beautiful that the poor fiddler must have known how little his own skill was worth. And it was this that tortured him worse than the fatigue.

"He who plays upon my violin understands the art. But never in all my born days have I been anything but a bungler. Now for the first time I 'm learning how music should sound."

For a few seconds he became so transported by the music that he forgot his evil fate; then he felt how his arm ached from weariness and he was seized anew with despair.

"This violin I cannot lay down until I have played myself to death. I can understand that the Water-Sprite won't be satisfied with less."

He began to weep over himself, but all the while he kept on playing.

"It would have been better for me had I stayed at home in the little cabin with mother. What is all the glory worth if it is to end in this way?"

He sat there hour after hour. Morning came on, the sun rose, and the birds sang all around him; but he played and he played, without intermission.

As it was a Sunday that dawned, he had to sit there by the old mill all alone. No human beings tramped in this part of the forest. They went to church down in the dale, and to the villages along the big highway.

Forenoon came along, and the sun stepped

higher and higher in the sky. The birds grew silent, and the wind began to murmur in the long pine needles.

Lars Larsson did not let the summer day's heat deter him. He played and played. At last evening was ushered in, the sun sank, but his bow needed no rest, and his arm continued to move.

"It is absolutely certain that this will be the death of me!" said he. "And it is a righteous punishment for all my conceit."

Far along in the evening a human being came wandering through the wood. It was a poor old woman with bent back and white hair, and a countenance that was furrowed by many sorrows.

"It seems strange," thought the player, "but I think I recognize that old woman. Can it be possible that it is my mother? Can it be possible that mother has grown so old and gray?"

He called aloud and stopped her. "Mother, mother, come here to me!" he cried.

She paused, as if unwillingly. "I hear now with my own ears that you are the best musician in Vermland," said she. "I can well understand that you do not care any more for a poor old woman like me!"

"Mother, mother, don't pass me by!" cried Lars Larsson. "I'm no great performer — only a poor wretch. Come here that I may speak with you!"

Then the mother came nearer and saw how he sat and played. His face was as pale as death, his hair dripped sweat, and blood oozed out from under the roots of his nails.

"Mother, I have fallen into misfortune because of my vanity, and now I must play myself to death. But tell me, before this happens, if you can forgive me, who left you alone and poor in your old age!"

His mother was seized with a great compassion for the son, and all the anger she had felt toward him was as if blown away. "Why, surely I forgive you!" said she. And as she saw his anguish and bewilderment and wanted him to understand that she meant what she said, she repeated it in the name of God.

"In the name of God our Redeemer, I forgive you!"

And when she said this, the bow stopped, the violin fell to the ground, and the musician arose saved and redeemed. For the enchantment was broken, because his old mother had felt such compassion for his distress that she had spoken God's name over him.

The Legend of the Christmas Rose

The Legend of the
Christmas Rose

ROBBER MOTHER, who lived in Robbers' Cave
up in Göinge forest, went down to the village
one day on a begging tour. Robber Father,
who was an outlawed man, did not dare to
leave the forest, but had to content himself
with lying in wait for the wayfarers who ventured within its borders. But at that time
travellers were not very plentiful in Southern
Skåne. If it so happened that the man had had
a few weeks of ill luck with his hunt, his wife
would take to the road. She took with her five
youngsters, and each youngster wore a ragged
leathern suit and birch-bark shoes and bore a
sack on his back as long as himself. When Robber Mother stepped inside the door of a cabin,
no one dared refuse to give her whatever she
demanded; for she was not above coming back
the following night and setting fire to the
house if she had not been well received. Robber
Mother and her brood were worse than a pack

of wolves, and many a man felt like running a spear through them; but it was never done, because they all knew that the man stayed up in the forest, and he would have known how to wreak vengeance if anything had happened to the children or the old woman.

Now that Robber Mother went from house to house and begged, she came one day to Övid, which at that time was a cloister. She rang the bell of the cloister gate and asked for food. The watchman let down a small wicket in the gate and handed her six round bread cakes — one for herself and one for each of the five children.

While the mother was standing quietly at the gate, her youngsters were running about. And now one of them came and pulled at her skirt, as a signal that he had discovered something which she ought to come and see, and Robber Mother followed him promptly.

The entire cloister was surrounded by a high and strong wall, but the youngster had managed to find a little back gate which stood ajar. When Robber Mother got there, she pushed the gate open and walked inside without asking leave, as it was her custom to do.

Övid Cloister was managed at that time by Abbot Hans, who knew all about herbs. Just within the cloister wall he had planted a little

herb garden, and it was into this that the old
woman had forced her way.

At first glance Robber Mother was so astonished that she paused at the gate. It was high
summertide, and Abbot Hans' garden was so
full of flowers that the eyes were fairly dazzled
by the blues, reds, and yellows, as one looked
into it. But presently an indulgent smile spread
over her features, and she started to walk up a
narrow path that lay between many flower-beds.

In the garden a lay brother walked about,
pulling up weeds. It was he who had left the
door in the wall open, that he might throw the
weeds and tares on the rubbish heap outside.

When he saw Robber Mother coming in, with
all five youngsters in tow, he ran toward her at
once and ordered them away. But the beggar
woman walked right on as before. She cast her
eyes up and down, looking now at the stiff white
lilies which spread near the ground, then on the
ivy climbing high upon the cloister wall, and
took no notice whatever of the lay brother.

He thought she had not understood him, and
wanted to take her by the arm and turn her
toward the gate. But when the robber woman
saw his purpose, she gave him a look that sent
him reeling backward. She had been walking
with back bent under her beggar's pack, but

now she straightened herself to her full height. "I am Robber Mother from Göinge forest; so touch me if you dare!" And it was obvious that she was as certain she would be left in peace as if she had announced that she was the Queen of Denmark.

And yet the lay brother dared to oppose her, although now, when he knew who she was, he spoke reasonably to her. "You must know, Robber Mother, that this is a monks' cloister, and no woman in the land is allowed within these walls. If you do not go away, the monks will be angry with me because I forgot to close the gate, and perhaps they will drive me away from the cloister and the herb garden."

But such prayers were wasted on Robber Mother. She walked straight ahead among the little flower-beds and looked at the hyssop with its magenta blossoms, and at the honeysuckles, which were full of deep orange-colored flower clusters.

Then the lay brother knew of no other remedy than to run into the cloister and call for help.

He returned with two stalwart monks, and Robber Mother saw that now it meant business! With feet firmly planted she stood in the path and began shrieking in strident tones all the awful vengeance she would wreak on the cloister if she

could n't remain in the herb garden as long as
she wished. But the monks did not see why
they need fear her and thought only of driving
her out. Then Robber Mother let out a perfect volley of shrieks, and, throwing herself
upon the monks, clawed and bit at them; so
did all the youngsters. The men soon learned
that she could overpower them, and all they
could do was to go back into the cloister for
reinforcements.

As they ran through the passage-way which
led to the cloister, they met Abbot Hans, who
came rushing out to learn what all this noise
was about.

Then they had to confess that Robber Mother
from Göinge forest had come into the cloister
and that they were unable to drive her out and
must call for assistance.

But Abbot Hans upbraided them for using
force and forbade their calling for help. He
sent both monks back to their work, and although he was an old and fragile man, he took
with him only the lay brother.

When Abbot Hans came out in the garden,
Robber Mother was still wandering among the
flower-beds. He regarded her with astonishment. He was certain that Robber Mother had
never before seen an herb garden; yet she saun-

tered leisurely between all the small patches, each of which had been planted with its own species of rare flower, and looked at them as if they were old acquaintances. At some she smiled, at others she shook her head.

Abbot Hans loved his herb garden as much as it was possible for him to love anything earthly and perishable. Wild and terrible as the old woman looked, he could n't help liking that she had fought with three monks for the privilege of viewing the garden in peace. He came up to her and asked in a mild tone if the garden pleased her.

. Robber Mother turned defiantly toward Abbot Hans, for she expected only to be trapped and overpowered. But when she noticed his white hair and bent form, she answered peaceably, "First, when I saw this, I thought I had never seen a prettier garden; but now I see that it can't be compared with one I know of."

Abbot Hans had certainly expected a different answer. When he heard that Robber Mother had seen a garden more beautiful than his, a faint flush spread over his withered cheek. The lay brother, who was standing close by, immediately began to censure the old woman. "This is Abbot Hans," said he, "who with much care and diligence has gathered the flowers from

far and near for his herb garden. We all know
that there is not a more beautiful garden to be
found in all Skåne, and it is not befitting that
you, who live in the wild forest all the year
around, should find fault with his work."

"I don't wish to make myself the judge of
either him or you," said Robber Mother. "I 'm
only saying that if you could see the garden of
which I am thinking you would uproot all the
flowers planted here and cast them away like
weeds."

But the Abbot's assistant was hardly less
proud of the flowers than the Abbot himself,
and after hearing her remarks he laughed de-
risively. "I can understand that you only talk
like this to tease us. It must be a pretty garden
that you have made for yourself amongst the
pines in Göinge forest! I 'd be willing to wager
my soul's salvation that you have never before
been within the walls of an herb garden."

Robber Mother grew crimson with rage to
think that her word was doubted, and she cried
out: "It may be true that until to-day I had
never been within the walls of an herb garden;
but you monks, who are holy men, certainly
must know that on every Christmas Eve the
great Göinge forest is transformed into a beautiful garden, to commemorate the hour of our

Lord's birth. We who live in the forest have seen this happen every year. And in that garden I have seen flowers so lovely that I dared not lift my hand to pluck them."

The lay brother wanted to continue the argument, but Abbot Hans gave him a sign to be silent. For, ever since his childhood, Abbot Hans had heard it said that on every Christmas Eve the forest was dressed in holiday glory. He had often longed to see it, but he had never had the good fortune. Eagerly he begged and implored Robber Mother that he might come up to the Robbers' Cave on Christmas Eve. If she would only send one of her children to show him the way, he could ride up there alone, and he would never betray them — on the contrary, he would reward them, in so far as it lay in his power.

Robber Mother said no at first, for she was thinking of Robber Father and of the peril which might befall him should she permit Abbot Hans to ride up to their cave. At the same time the desire to prove to the monk that the garden which she knew was more beautiful than his got the better of her, and she gave in.

"But more than one follower you cannot take with you," said she, "and you are not to waylay us or trap us, as sure as you are a holy man."

This Abbot Hans promised, and then Robber Mother went her way. Abbot Hans commanded the lay brother not to reveal to a soul that which had been agreed upon. He feared that the monks, should they learn of his purpose, would not allow a man of his years to go up to the Robbers' Cave.

Nor did he himself intend to reveal his project to a human being. And then it happened that Archbishop Absalon from Lund came to Övid and remained through the night. When Abbot Hans was showing him the herb garden, he got to thinking of Robber Mother's visit, and the lay brother, who was at work in the garden, heard Abbot Hans telling the Bishop about Robber Father, who these many years had lived as an outlaw in the forest, and asking him for a letter of ransom for the man, that he might lead an honest life among respectable folk. "As things are now," said Abbot Hans, "his children are growing up into worse malefactors than himself, and you will soon have a whole gang of robbers to deal with up there in the forest."

But the Archbishop replied that he did not care to let the robber loose among honest folk in the villages. It would be best for all that he remain in the forest.

Then Abbot Hans grew zealous and told the

Bishop all about Göinge forest, which, every year at Yuletide, clothed itself in summer bloom around the Robbers' Cave. "If these bandits are not so bad but that God's glories can be made manifest to them, surely we cannot be too wicked to experience the same blessing."

The Archbishop knew how to answer Abbot Hans. "This much I will promise you, Abbot Hans," he said, smiling, "that any day you send me a blossom from the garden in Göinge forest, I will give you letters of ransom for all the outlaws you may choose to plead for."

The lay brother apprehended that Bishop Absalon believed as little in this story of Robber Mother's as he himself; but Abbot Hans perceived nothing of the sort, but thanked Absalon for his good promise and said that he would surely send him the flower.

Abbot Hans had his way. And the following Christmas Eve he did not sit at home with his monks in Övid Cloister, but was on his way to Göinge forest. One of Robber Mother's wild youngsters ran ahead of him, and close behind him was the lay brother who had talked with Robber Mother in the herb garden.

Abbot Hans had been longing to make this journey, and he was very happy now that it had

come to pass. But it was a different matter with
the lay brother who accompanied him. Abbot
Hans was very dear to him, and he would not
willingly have allowed another to attend him
and watch over him; but he did n't believe that
he should see any Christmas Eve garden. He
thought the whole thing a snare which Robber
Mother had, with great cunning, laid for Abbot
Hans, that he might fall into her husband's
clutches.

While Abbot Hans was riding toward the
forest, he saw that everywhere they were preparing to celebrate Christmas. In every peasant
settlement fires were lighted in the bath-house
to warm it for the afternoon bathing. Great
hunks of meat and bread were being carried from
the larders into the cabins, and from the barns
came the men with big sheaves of straw to be
strewn over the floors.

As he rode by the little country churches, he
observed that each parson, with his sexton, was
busily engaged in decorating his church; and
when he came to the road which leads to Bösjo
Cloister, he observed that all the poor of the
parish were coming with armfuls of bread and
long candles, which they had received at the
cloister gate.

When (Abbot Hans) saw all these Christmas

preparations, his haste increased. He was thinking of the festivities that awaited him, which were greater than any the others would be privileged to enjoy.

But the lay brother whined and fretted when he saw how they were preparing to celebrate Christmas in every humble cottage. He grew more and more anxious, and begged and implored Abbot Hans to turn back and not to throw himself deliberately into the robber's hands.

Abbot Hans went straight ahead, paying no heed to his lamentations. He left the plain behind him and came up into desolate and wild forest regions. Here the road was bad, almost like a stony and burr-strewn path, with neither bridge nor plank to help them over brooklet and rivulet. The farther they rode, the colder it grew, and after a while they came upon snow-covered ground.

It turned out to be a long and hazardous ride through the forest. They climbed steep and slippery side paths, crawled over swamp and marsh, and pushed through windfall and bramble. Just as daylight was waning, the robber boy guided them across a forest meadow, skirted by tall, naked leaf trees and green fir trees. Back of the meadow loomed a mountain wall, and in this wall they saw a door of thick boards. Now Abbot Hans understood that they had arrived, and dismounted. The child opened the heavy door for him, and he looked into a poor mountain grotto, with bare stone walls. Robber Mother was seated before a log fire that burned in the middle of the floor. Alongside the walls were beds of virgin pine and moss, and on one of these beds lay Robber Father asleep.

"Come in, you out there!" shouted Robber Mother without rising, "and fetch the horses in with you, so they won't be destroyed by the night cold."

Abbot Hans walked boldly into the cave, and the lay brother followed. Here were wretchedness and poverty! and nothing was done to celebrate Christmas. Robber Mother had neither brewed nor baked; she had neither washed nor scoured. The youngsters were lying on the floor around a kettle, eating; but no better food was provided for them than a watery gruel.

Robber Mother spoke in a tone as haughty and dictatorial as any well-to-do peasant woman. "Sit down by the fire and warm yourself, Abbot Hans," said she; "and if you have food with you, eat, for the food which we in the forest prepare you would n't care to taste. And if you are tired after the long journey, you can lie down on one of these beds to sleep. You need n't be afraid of oversleeping, for I 'm sitting here by the fire keeping watch. I shall awaken you in time to see that which you have come up here to see."

Abbot Hans obeyed Robber Mother and brought forth his food sack; but he was so fatigued after the journey he was hardly able to eat, and as soon as he could stretch himself on the bed, he fell asleep.

The lay brother was also assigned a bed to rest upon, but he did n't dare sleep, as he thought he had better keep his eye on Robber Father to prevent his getting up and capturing Abbot Hans. But gradually fatigue got the better of him, too, and he dropped into a doze.

When he woke up, he saw that Abbot Hans had left his bed and was sitting by the fire talking with Robber Mother. The outlawed robber sat also by the fire. He was a tall, raw-boned man with a dull, sluggish appearance. His back was turned to Abbot Hans, as though he would have it appear that he was not listening to the conversation.

Abbot Hans was telling Robber Mother all about the Christmas preparations he had seen on the journey, reminding her of Christmas feasts and games which she must have known in her youth, when she lived at peace with mankind. "I'm sorry for your children, who can never run on the village street in holiday dress or tumble in the Christmas straw," said he.

At first Robber Mother answered in short, gruff sentences, but by degrees she became more subdued and listened more intently. Suddenly Robber Father turned toward Abbot Hans and shook his clenched fist in his face. "You miserable monk! did you come here to coax from me my wife and children? Don't you know that I am an outlaw and may not leave the forest?"

Abbot Hans looked him fearlessly in the eyes. "It is my purpose to get a letter of ransom for you from Archbishop Absalon," said he. He had hardly finished speaking when the robber and his wife burst out laughing. They knew well enough the kind of mercy a forest robber could expect from Bishop Absalon!

"Oh, if I get a letter of ransom from Absalon," said Robber Father, "then I'll promise you that never again will I steal so much as a goose."

The lay brother was annoyed with the robber folk for daring to laugh at Abbot Hans, but on his own account he was well pleased. He had seldom seen the Abbot sitting more peaceful and meek with his monks at Övid than he now sat with this wild robber folk.

Suddenly Robber Mother rose. "You sit here and talk, Abbot Hans," she said, "so that we are forgetting to look at the forest. Now I can hear, even in this cave, how the Christmas bells are ringing."

The words were barely uttered when they all sprang up and rushed out. But in the forest it was still dark night and bleak winter. The only thing they marked was a distant clang borne on a light south wind.

"How can this bell ringing ever awaken the dead forest?" thought Abbot Hans. For now, as he stood out in the winter darkness, he thought it far more impossible that a summer garden could spring up here than it had seemed to him before.

When the bells had been ringing a few moments, a sudden illumination penetrated the forest; the next moment it was dark again, and then the light came back. It pushed its way forward between the stark trees, like a shimmering mist. This much it effected: The darkness merged into a faint daybreak. Then Abbot Hans saw that the snow had vanished from the ground, as if some one had removed a carpet, and the earth began to take on a green covering. Then the ferns shot up their fronds, rolled like a bishop's staff. The heather that grew on the stony hills and the bog-myrtle rooted in the

ground moss dressed themselves quickly in new
bloom. The moss-tufts thickened and raised
themselves, and the spring blossoms shot upward
their swelling buds, which already had a touch
of color.

Abbot Hans' heart beat fast as he marked the
first signs of the forest's awakening. "Old man
that I am, shall I behold such a miracle?"
thought he, and the tears wanted to spring to his
eyes. Again it grew so hazy that he feared the
darkness would once more cover the earth; but
almost immediately there came a new wave of
light. It brought with it the splash of rivulet and
the rush of cataract. Then the leaves of the trees
burst into bloom, as if a swarm of green butterflies came flying and clustered on the branches.
It was not only trees and plants that awoke. but
crossbeaks hopped from branch to branch, and
the woodpeckers hammered on the limbs until
the splinters fairly flew around them. A flock
of starlings from up country lighted in a fir top
to rest. They were paradise starlings. The tips
of each tiny feather shone in brilliant reds, and,
as the·birds moved, they glittered like so many
jewels.

Again, all was dark for an instant, but soon
there came a new light wave. A fresh, warm
south wind blew and scattered over the forest

meadow all the little seeds that had been brought here from southern lands by birds and ships and winds, and which could not thrive elsewhere because of this country's cruel cold. These took root and sprang up the instant they touched the ground.

When the next warm wind came along, the blueberries and lignon ripened. Cranes and wild geese shrieked in the air, the bullfinches built nests, and the baby squirrels began playing on the branches of the trees.

Everything came so fast now that Abbot Hans could not stop to reflect on how immeasurably great was the miracle that was taking place. He had time only to use his eyes and ears. The next light wave that came rushing in brought with it the scent of newly ploughed acres, and far off in the distance the milkmaids were heard coaxing the cows — and the tinkle of the sheep's bells. Pine and spruce trees were so thickly clothed with red cones that they shone like crimson mantles. The juniper berries changed color every second, and forest flowers covered the ground till it was all red, blue, and yellow.

Abbot Hans bent down to the earth and broke off a wild strawberry blossom, and, as he straightened up, the berry ripened in his hand.

The mother fox came out of her lair with a big

litter of black-legged young. She went up to
Robber Mother and scratched at her skirt, and
Robber Mother bent down to her and praised
her young. The horned owl, who had just begun
his night chase, was astonished at the light and
went back to his ravine to perch for the night.
The male cuckoo crowed, and his mate stole up
to the nests of the little birds with her egg in her
mouth.

Robber Mother's youngsters let out perfect
shrieks of delight. They stuffed themselves with
wild strawberries that hung on the bushes, large
as pine cones. One of them played with a litter
of young hares; another ran a race with some
young crows, which had hopped from their nest
before they were really ready; a third caught up
an adder from the ground and wound it around
his neck and arm.

Robber Father was standing out on a marsh
eating raspberries. When he glanced up, a big
black bear stood beside him. Robber Father
broke off an osier twig and struck the bear on
the nose. "Keep to your own ground, you!"
he said; "this is my turf." Then the huge bear
turned around and lumbered off in another
direction.

New waves of warmth and light kept coming,
and now they brought with them seeds from the

star-flower. Golden pollen from rye fields fairly
flew in the air. Then came butterflies, so big
that they looked like flying lilies. The bee-hive
in a hollow oak was already so full of honey that
it dripped down on the trunk of the tree. Then
all the flowers whose seeds had been brought
from foreign lands began to blossom. The love-
liest roses climbed up the mountain wall in a
race with the blackberry vines, and from the
forest meadow sprang flowers as large as human
faces.

Abbot Hans thought of the flower he was to
pluck for Bishop Absalon; but each new flower
that appeared was more beautiful than the
others, and he wanted to choose the most beautiful of all.

Wave upon wave kept coming until the air was
so filled with light that it glittered. All the life
and beauty and joy of summer smiled on Abbot
Hans. He felt that earth could bring no greater
happiness than that which welled up about him,
and he said to himself, "I do not know what new
beauties the next wave that comes can bring
with it."

But the light kept streaming in, and now it
seemed to Abbot Hans that it carried with it
something from an infinite distance. He felt a
celestial atmosphere enfolding him, and trem-

blingly he began to anticipate, now that earth's joys had come, the glories of heaven were approaching.

Then Abbot Hans marked how all grew still; the birds hushed their songs, the flowers ceased growing, and the young foxes played no more. The glory now nearing was such that the heart wanted to stop beating; the eyes wept without one's knowing it; the soul longed to soar away into the Eternal. From far in the distance faint harp tones were heard, and celestial song, like a soft murmur, reached him.

Abbot Hans clasped his hands and dropped to his knees. His face was radiant with bliss. Never had he dreamed that even in this life it should be granted him to taste the joys of heaven, and to hear angels sing Christmas carols!

But beside Abbot Hans stood the lay brother who had accompanied him. In his mind there were dark thoughts. "This cannot be a true miracle," he thought, "since it is revealed to malefactors. This does not come from God, but has its origin in witchcraft and is sent hither by Satan. It is the Evil One's power that is tempting us and compelling us to see that which has no real existence."

From afar were heard the sound of angel harps

and the tones of a Miserere. But the lay brother thought it was the evil spirits of hell coming closer. "They would enchant and seduce us," sighed he, "and we shall be sold into perdition."

The angel throng was so near now that Abbot Hans saw their bright forms through the forest branches. The lay brother saw them, too; but back of all this wondrous beauty he saw only some dread evil. For him it was the devil who performed these wonders on the anniversary of our Saviour's birth. It was done simply for the purpose of more effectually deluding poor human beings.

All the while the birds had been circling around the head of Abbot Hans, and they let him take them in his hands. But all the animals were afraid of the lay brother; no bird perched on his shoulder, no snake played at his feet. Then there came a little forest dove. When she marked that the angels were nearing, she plucked up courage and flew down on the lay brother's shoulder and laid her head against his cheek.

Then it appeared to him as if sorcery were come right upon him, to tempt and corrupt him. He struck with his hand at the forest dove and cried in such a loud voice that it rang throughout the forest, "Go thou back to hell, whence thou art come!"

Just then the angels were so near that Abbot Hans felt the feathery touch of their great wings, and he bowed down to earth in reverent greeting.

But when the lay brother's words sounded, their song was hushed and the holy guests turned in flight. ⌐ At the same time the light and the mild warmth vanished in unspeakable terror for the darkness and cold in a human heart. Darkness sank over the earth, like a coverlet; frost came, all the growths shrivelled up; the animals and birds hastened away; the rushing of streams was hushed; the leaves dropped from the trees, rustling like rain.

Abbot Hans felt how his heart, which had but lately swelled with bliss, was now contracting with insufferable agony. "I can never outlive this," thought he, "that the angels from heaven had been so close to me and were driven away; that they wanted to sing Christmas carols for me and were driven to flight."

Then he remembered the flower he had promised Bishop Absalon, and at the last moment he fumbled among the leaves and moss to try and find a blossom. But he sensed how the ground under his fingers froze and how the white snow came gliding over the ground. Then his heart caused him ever greater anguish. He could not rise, but fell prostrate on the ground and lay there.

When the robber folk and the lay brother had groped their way back to the cave, they missed Abbot Hans. They took brands with them and went out to search for him. They found him dead upon the coverlet of snow.

Then the lay brother began weeping and lamenting, for he understood that it was he who had killed Abbot Hans because he had dashed from him the cup of happiness which he had been thirsting to drain to its last drop.

When Abbot Hans had been carried down to Övid, those who took charge of the dead saw that he held his right hand locked tight around something which he must have grasped at the moment of death. When they finally got his hand open, they found that the thing which he had held in such an iron grip was a pair of white root bulbs, which he had torn from among the moss and leaves.

When the lay brother who had accompanied Abbot Hans saw the bulbs, he took them and planted them in Abbot Hans' herb garden.

He guarded them the whole year to see if any flower would spring from them. But in vain he waited through the spring, the summer, and the autumn. Finally, when winter had set in and all the leaves and the flowers were dead, he ceased caring for them.

But when Christmas Eve came again, he was so strongly reminded of Abbot Hans that he wandered out into the garden to think of him. And look! as he came to the spot where he had planted the bare root bulbs, he saw that from them had sprung flourishing green stalks, which bore beautiful flowers with silver white leaves.

He called out all the monks at Övid, and when they saw that this plant bloomed on Christmas Eve, when all the other growths were as if dead, they understood that this flower had in truth been plucked by Abbot Hans from the Christmas garden in Göinge forest. Then the lay brother asked the monks if he might take a few blossoms to Bishop Absalon.

And when he appeared before Bishop Absalon, he gave him the flowers and said: "Abbot Hans sends you these. They are the flowers he promised to pick for you from the garden in Göinge forest."

When Bishop Absalon beheld the flowers, which had sprung from the earth in darkest winter, and heard the words, he turned as pale as if he had met a ghost. He sat in silence a moment; thereupon he said, "Abbot Hans has faithfully kept his word and I shall also keep mine." And he ordered that a letter of ransom be drawn up for the wild robber who was outlawed and had been forced to live in the forest ever since his youth.

He handed the letter to the lay brother, who departed at once for the Robbers' Cave. When he stepped in there on Christmas Day, the robber came toward him with axe uplifted. "I'd like to hack you monks into bits, as many as you are!" said he. "It must be your fault that Göinge forest did not last night dress itself in Christmas bloom."

"The fault is mine alone," said the lay brother, "and I will gladly die for it; but first I must deliver a message from Abbot Hans." And he drew forth the Bishop's letter and told the man that he was free. "Hereafter you and your children shall play in the Christmas straw and celebrate your Christmas among people, just as Abbot Hans wished to have it," said he.

Then Robber Father stood there pale and speechless, but Robber Mother said in his name, "Abbot Hans has indeed kept his word, and Robber Father will keep his."

When the robber and his wife left the cave, the lay brother moved in and lived all alone in the forest, in constant meditation and prayer that his hard-heartedness might be forgiven him.

But Göinge forest never again celebrated the hour of our Saviour's birth; and of all its glory, there lives to-day only the plant which Abbot Hans had plucked. It has been named CHRISTMAS ROSE. And each year at Christmastide she sends forth from the earth her green stalks and white blossoms, as if she never could forget that she had once grown in the great Christmas garden at Göinge forest.

A Story from Jerusalem

A Story from Jerusalem

IN the old and time-honored mosque, El Aksa, in Jerusalem, there is a long, winding path leading from the main entrance up to a very deep and wide window-niche. In this niche a very old and much worn rug is spread; and upon this rug, day in and day out, sits old Mesullam, who is a fortune-teller and dream-interpreter, and who for a paltry penny serves the visitors to the mosque by prying into their future destinies.

It happened one afternoon, several years ago, that Mesullam, who sat as usual in his window, was so ill-natured that he would n't even return the greetings of the passers-by. No one thought, however, of feeling offended at his rudeness, because every one knew that he was grieving over a humiliation which had been put upon him that day.

At that time a mighty monarch from the Occident was visiting Jerusalem, and in the forenoon the distinguished stranger with his retinue had wandered through El Aksa. Before his arrival the superintendent of the mosque

had commanded the servants to scour and
dust all the nooks and corners of the old building, at the same time giving orders that
Mesullam should move out of his accustomed
place. He had found that it would be simply
impossible to let him remain there during
the visit of the distinguished guest. It was
not only that his rug was very ragged, or that
he had piled up around him a lot of dirty sacks
in which he kept his belongings, but Mesullam
himself was anything but an ornament to the
mosque! He was, in reality, an inconceivably
ugly old negro. His lips were enormous, his
chin protruded aggressively, his brow was
exceedingly low, and his nose was almost like a
snout; and in addition to these, Mesullam had a
coarse and wrinkled skin and a clumsy, thick-
set body, which was carelessly draped in a dirty
white shawl. So one can't wonder that he was
forbidden to show himself in the mosque while
the honored guest was there!

Poor Mesullam, who knew well enough that,
despite his ugliness, he was a very wise man,
experienced a bitter disappointment in that *he*
was not to see the royal traveller. He had hoped
that he might give him some proofs of the great
accomplishments which he possessed in occult
things and in this way add to his own glory and

renown. Since this hope had miscarried, he sat hour after hour in a queer position, and mourned, with his long arms stretched upward and his head thrown far back, as though he were calling upon heaven for justice.

When it drew on toward evening, Mesullam was wakened from his state of all-absorbing grief by a cheery voice calling him. It was a Syrian who, accompanied by another traveller, had come up to the soothsayer. He told him that the stranger whom he was conducting wished for a proof of Oriental wisdom, and that he had spoken to him of Mesullam's ability to interpret dreams.

Mesullam answered not a word to this, but maintained his former attitude rigidly. When the guide asked him again if he would not listen to the dreams the stranger wished to relate to him and interpret them, his arms dropped and he crossed them on his breast. Assuming the attitude of a wronged man, he answered that this evening his soul was so filled with his own troubles that he could n't judge anything clearly which concerned another.

But the stranger, who had a buoyant and commanding personality, did n't seem to mind his objections. As there was no chair handy, he kicked aside the rug and seated himself in the window-niche. Then he began, in a clear and vibrant voice, to narrate a few dreams, which later were translated for the soothsayer by the guide.

"Tell him," said the traveller, "that a few years ago I was at Cairo, in Egypt. Since he is a learned man, naturally he knows there is a mosque there, called El Azhar, which is the most celebrated institution of learning in the Orient. I went there one day to visit it, and found that the whole colossal structure — all its rooms and arcades, all its entrances and halls were filled with students. There were old men who had devoted their entire lives to the quest for knowledge, and children who were just learning to form their letters. There were giantesque negroes from the heart of Africa; lithe, handsome youths from India and Arabia; far-travelled strangers from Barbary, from Georgia, from every land where the natives embrace the doctrines of the Koran. Close to the pillars — I was told that in El Azhar there were as many teachers as there were pillars — the instructors were squatted on their rugs, while their students, who were arranged in a circle around them, eagerly followed their lectures, which were accompanied by swaying movements of their bodies. And tell him that, although El Azhar is in no way comparable to the great Occidental seats of learning, I was nevertheless astonished at what I saw there. I remarked to myself: 'Ah, this is Islam's great stronghold and defence! From here Mohammed's young champions go out. Here, at El Azhar, the potions of wisdom that keep the Koran's doctrines healthy and vigorous are blended.'"

All of this the traveller said almost in one breath. Now he made a pause, so that the guide would have an opportunity to interpret for the soothsayer. Then he continued:

"Now tell him that El Azhar made such a powerful impression upon me that on the following night I saw it again in a dream. I saw the white marble structure and the many students dressed in white mantles and white turbans — as is the custom at El Azhar. I wandered through halls and courts and was again astonished at what a splendid fortress and wall of protection this was for Mohammedanism. Finally — in the dream — I came to the minaret upon which the prayer-crier stands to inform the faithful that the hour of prayer has struck. And I saw the stairway which winds up to the minaret, and I saw a prayer-crier walking up the steps. He wore a black mantle and a white

turban, like the others, and as he went up the
stairs I could not at first see his face, but when
he had made a few turns on the spiral stairway,
he happened to turn his face toward me, and
then I saw that it was *Christ*."

The speaker made a short pause, and his chest
was expanded for a deep inhalation. "I shall
never forget, although it was only a dream,"
he exclaimed, "what an impression it made
upon me to see Christ walking up the steps to
the minaret in El Azhar! To me it seemed so
glorious and significant that he had come to this
stronghold of Islam to call out the hours of
prayer that I leaped up in the dream and
awaked."

Here the traveller made another pause to let
the guide interpret for the soothsayer. But
this appeared to be well-nigh useless labor.
Mesullam sat all the while, with his hands on
his sides, rocking back and forth, and with his
eyes half closed. He seemed to want to say:
"Inasmuch as I cannot escape these importunate
people, at least I will let them see that I don't
care to listen to what they have to say. I'll
try and rock myself to sleep. It will be the
best way to show them how little I care about
them."

The guide intimated to the traveller that all

their trouble would be in vain and they would n't hear a sensible word from Mesullam while he was in this mood. But the European stranger seemed to be entranced by Mesullam's indescribable ugliness and extraordinary behavior. He looked at him with the pleasure of a child when it is watching a wild animal in a menagerie, and he desired to continue the interview.

"Tell him that I would n't have troubled him to interpret this dream," he said, "had it not, in a certain sense, come to me again. Let him know that two weeks ago I visited the Sophia' Mosque at Constantinople, and that I, after wandering through this magnificent building, stepped up on a minaret in order to get a better view of the auditorium. Tell him, also, that they allowed me to come into the mosque during a service, when it was filled with people. Upon each of the innumerable prayer rugs which covered the whole floor of the main hall, a man was standing and saying his prayers. All who took part in the service simultaneously made the same movements. All fell upon their knees and threw themselves on their faces and raised themselves, at the same time whispering their prayers very low; but from the almost imperceptible movements of so many lips came a mysterious murmur, which rose toward the high arches and died away, time and again. Then there came melodious responses from remote passages and galleries. It was so strange altogether that one wondered if it was not the Spirit of God that poured into the old sanctuary."

The traveller made another pause. He observed Mesullam carefully, while the guide interpreted his speech. It actually appeared as if he had tried to win the negro's approbation with his eloquence. And it seemed, too, as though he would succeed, for Mesullam's half-closed eyes flashed once, like a coal that is beginning to take fire. But the soothsayer, stubborn as a child that will not let itself be amused, dropped his head on his breast and began an even more impatient rocking of his body.

"Tell him," resumed the stranger, "tell him that I have never seen people pray with such fervor! To me it seemed as if it was the sublime beauty of this marvellous structure which created this atmosphere of ecstasy. Verily this is still an Islam bulwark! This is the home of devoutness! From this great mosque emanate the faith and enthusiasm which make Islam a mighty power."

Here he paused again, noting carefully Mesullam's play of features during its interpretation.

Not a trace of interest was discernible in them. But the stranger was evidently a man who liked to hear himself talk. His own words intoxicated him; he would have become ill-natured had he not been allowed to proceed.

"Well," said he, when it was his turn again to speak, "I cannot rightly explain what happened to me. Possibly the faint odor from the hundreds of oil lamps, together with the low murmurings of the devotees, lulled me into a kind of stupefaction. I could not help but close my eyes as I stood leaning against a pillar. Soon sleep, or rather insensibility, overcame me. Probably it did not last more than a minute, but during this interval I was entirely removed from reality. While in this trance I could see the whole Sophia Mosque before me, with all the praying people; but now I saw what I had not hitherto observed. Up in the dome were scaffoldings, and on these stood a number of workmen with paint pots and brushes.

"Tell him, if he does not already know it," continued the narrator, "that Sophia Mosque was once a Christian church, and that its arches and dome are covered with sacred Christian mosaics, although the Turks have painted out all these pictures with plain yellow paint. And it appeared to me as if the yellow paint in the dome had peeled off in a couple of places and that the painters had clambered up on the scaffolding to touch up the picture. But, look! when one of them raised his brush to fill in the color, another large piece scaled off, and suddenly one saw from behind it a beautiful painting of the *Christ* emerge. Again the painter raised his arm to paint out the picture, but the arm, which appeared to be numb and powerless, dropped down before this beautiful face; at the same time the paint dropped from the entire dome and arch, and Christ was visible there in all his glory, among angels and heavenly hosts. Then the painter cried out, and all the worshippers down on the floor of the mosque raised their heads. And when they saw the heavenly hosts surrounding the Saviour, they sent up a cry of joy, and when I witnessed this joy, I was seized with such strong emotion that I waked instantly. Then everything was like itself. The mosaics were hidden under the yellow paint and the devotees continued all the while to invoke Allah."

When the interpreter had translated this, Mesullam opened one eye and regarded the stranger. He saw a man who he thought resembled all other Occidentals that wandered through the mosque. "I don't believe the pale-

faced stranger has seen any visions," thought
he. "He has not the dark eyes that can see what
is behind the veil of mystery. I think, rather,
that he came here to make sport of me. I must
beware lest on this accursed day I be overtaken
by another humiliation."

The stranger spoke anon: "You know, O
Dream Interpreter!" turning now direct to
Mesullam, as if he thought that he could understand him, despite his foreign tongue — "you
know that a distinguished foreigner is visiting
Jerusalem at present, and on his account they
have talked of opening the walled-up gate in
Jerusalem's ring-wall — the one they call 'the
Golden' and which is believed to be the gate
through which Jesus rode into Jerusalem on
Palm Sunday. They have actually been thinking of doing the distinguished traveller the honor
of letting him ride into the city through a gate
which has been walled up for centuries; but they
were held back by an old prophecy which
foretells that when this gate is opened the Occidentals will march in through it to take
possession of Jerusalem.

"And now you shall hear what happened to
me last night. The weather was superb; it
was glorious moonlight, and I had gone out
alone to take a quiet promenade around the Holy

City. I walked outside the ring-wall on the narrow path that extends all round the wall, and my thoughts were borne so far back into distant ages that I scarcely remembered where I was. All of a sudden I began to feel tired. I wondered if I should not soon come to a gate in the wall, through which I might get into the city and thus return to my quarters by a shorter road. Well, just as I was thinking of this, I saw a man open a large gate in the wall directly in front of me. He opened it wide and beckoned to me that I might pass in through it. I was absorbed in my dreams and hardly knew how far I had been walking. I was somewhat surprised that there was a gate here, but I thought no more about the matter and walked through it. As soon as I had passed through the deep archway, the gate closed with a sharp clang. When I turned round, there was no opening visible, only a walled-up gate — the one called the Golden. Before me lay the temple place, the broad Haram plateau, in the centre of which Omar's Mosque is enthroned. And you know that no gate in the ring-wall leads thither but the Golden, which is not only closed but walled up.

"You can understand that I thought I'd gone mad; that I dreamed I had tried in vain to

find some explanation of this. I looked around
for the man who had let me in. He had vanished and I could not find him. But, on the other
hand, I saw him all the plainer in memory —
the tall and slightly bent figure, the beautiful
locks, the mild visage, the parted beard. It
was *Christ*, soothsayer, *Christ* once again.

"Tell me now, you who can look into the hidden, what mean my dreams? What, more than
all, can be the meaning of my having really and
truly passed through the Golden Gate? Even
at this moment I do not know how it happened,
but I have done so. Tell me, now, what these
three things can mean!"

The interpreter translated this for Mesullam,
but the soothsayer was all the while in the same
suspicious and crabbed mood. "I am certain
that this stranger wants to poke fun at me," he
thought. "Perchance he would provoke me to
anger with all this talk about Christ?"

He would have concluded not to answer at
all; but when the interpreter insisted, he muttered a few words.

"What does he say?" asked the traveller
eagerly.

"He says he has nothing to say to you but
that dreams are dreams."

"Then tell him from me," retorted the

stranger, somewhat exasperated, "that this is not always true. It depends entirely upon who dreams them."

Before these words had been interpreted to Mesullam, the European had arisen and with quick and elastic step had walked toward the long passage-way.

But Mesullam sat still and mused over his answer for five minutes. Then he fell upon his face, utterly undone. "Allah, Allah! Twice on the same day Fortune has passed by me without my having captured her. What hath thy servant done to displease thee?"

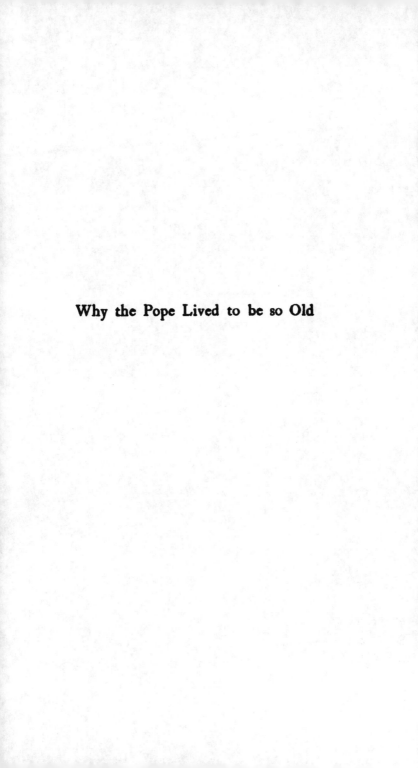

Why the Pope Lived to be so Old

Why the Pope Lived to
be so Old

IT happened at Rome in the early nineties.
Leo XIII was just then at the height of his
fame and greatness. All true Catholics re-
joiced at his successes and triumphs, which in
truth were sublime. And, even for those who
could not grasp the great political events, it was
plain that the power of the Church was again
coming to the front. Any one at all could see
that new cloisters were going up everywhere and
that throngs of pilgrims were beginning to pour
into Italy, as in olden times. In many, many
places one saw the old, dilapidated churches in
process of restoration, damaged mosaics being
put in order, and the treasure-vaults of the
churches being filled with golden relic-boxes and
jewelled exhibits.

Right in the midst of this progressive period
the Roman people were alarmed by the news that
the Pope had been taken ill. He was said to be
in a very precarious condition; it was even
rumored that he was dying.

His condition was, too, in a great degree serious. The Pope's physicians issued bulletins which inspired but little hope. It was maintained that the Pope's great age — he was then ninety years old — made it seem almost incredible that he could survive this attack.

Naturally, the Pope's illness caused great unrest. In all the churches in Rome prayers were said for his recovery. The newspapers were filled with communications regarding the progress of the illness. The Cardinals were beginning to take steps and measures for the new Papal election.

Everywhere they bemoaned the approaching demise of the brilliant leader. They feared that the good fortune which had followed the Church's standard under Leo XIII might not be faithful to it under the leadership of his successor. There were many who had hoped that this Pope would succeed in winning back Rome and the Ecclesiastical States. Others, again, had dreamed that he would bring back into the bosom of the Church some of the large Protestant countries.

For each second that was passing, fear and anxiety grew apace. As night came on, in many homes the inmates would not retire. The churches were kept open until long past midnight, that the anxious ones might have an opportunity to go in and pray.

Among these throngs of devotees there was certainly more than one poor soul who cried out: "Dear Lord, take my life instead of his! Let him, who has done so much for Thy glory, live, and extinguish instead my life-flame, which burns to no one's use!"

But if the Angel of Death had taken one of these devotees at his word and had suddenly stepped up to him, with sword raised, to exact the fulfilment of his promise, one might wonder somewhat as to how he would have behaved. No doubt he would have recalled instantly such a rash proffer and begged for the grace of being allowed to live out all the years of his allotted time.

At this time there lived an old woman in one of the dingy ramshackle houses along the Tiber. She was one of those who have the kind of spirit that thanks God every day for life. Every morning she used to sit at the market-place and sell garden truck. And this was an occupation that was very congenial to her. She thought nothing could be livelier than a market of a morning. All tongues were wagging — all were harking their commodities, and buyers crowded in front of the stalls, selected and bargained, and many a good sally passed between buyer and seller. Sometimes the old woman was successful in making a good deal and in selling out her entire stock; but even if she could n't sell so much as a radish, she loved to be standing amongst flowers and green things in the fresh morning air.

In the evening she had another and an even greater pleasure. Then her son came home and visited with her. He was a priest, but he had been assigned to a little church in one of the humble quarters. The poor priests who served there had not much to live upon, and the mother feared that her son was starving. But from this, also, she derived much pleasure, for it gave her the opportunity of stuffing him full of delicacies when he came to see her. He struggled against it, as he was destined for a life of self-denial and strict discipline, but his mother became so distressed when he said no that he always had to give in. While he was eating she trotted around in the room and chattered about all that she had seen in the morning during market hours. These were all very worldly matters, and it would occur to her sometimes that her son might be offended. Then she would break off in the middle of a sentence and begin to talk of spiritual and solemn things, but the priest could n't help laughing. "No, no, mother Concenza!" he said, "continue in your usual way. The saints know you already, and they know what you are up to."

Then she, too, laughed and said: "You are quite right. It does n't pay to pretend before the good Lord."

When the Pope was taken ill, Signora Concenza must also have a share in the general grief. Of her own accord it certainly never would have occurred to her to feel troubled about his passing. But when her son came home to her, she could neither persuade him to taste of a morsel of food nor to give her a smile, although she was simply bubbling over with stories and interpolations. Naturally she became alarmed and asked what was wrong with him. "The Holy Father is ill," answered the son.

At first she could scarcely believe that this was the cause of his downheartedness. Of course it was a sorrow; but she knew, to be sure, that if a Pope died, immediately there would come another. She reminded her son of the fact that they had also mourned the good Pio Nono. And, you see, the one who succeeded him was a still greater Pope. Surely the Cardinals would choose for them a ruler who was just as holy and wise as this one.

The priest then began telling her about the Pope. He did n't bother to initiate her into his system of government, but he told her little stories of his childhood and young manhood. And from the days of his prelacy there were also things to relate — as, for instance, how he had at one time hunted down robbers in southern Italy, how he had made himself beloved by the poor and needy during the years when he was a bishop in Perugia.

Her eyes filled with tears, and she cried out: "Ah, if he were not so old! If he might only be allowed to live many more years, since he is such a great and holy man!"

"Ah, if only he were not so old!" sighed the son.

But Signora Concenza had already brushed the tears from her eyes. "You really must bear this calmly," said she. "Remember that his years of life are simply run out. It is impossible to prevent death from seizing him."

The priest was a dreamer. He loved the Church and had dreamed that the great Pope would lead her on to important and decisive victories. "I would give my life if I could purchase new life for him!" said he.

"What are you saying?" cried his mother. "Do you really love him so much? But, in any case, you must not express such dangerous wishes. Instead, you should think of living a good long time. Who knows what may happen? Why could n't you, in your turn, become Pope ? "

A' night and a day passed without any improvement in the Pope's condition. When Signora Concenza met her son the following day, he looked completely undone. She understood that he had passed the whole day in prayer and fasting, and she began to feel deeply grieved. "I verily believe that you mean to kill yourself for the sake of that sick old man ! " said she.

The son was hurt by again finding her without sympathy, and tried to persuade her to sympathize a little with his grief. "You, truly, more than any one else, ought to wish that the Pope might live," he said. "If he may continue to rule, he will name my parish priest for bishop before the year shall have passed and, in that event, my fortune is made. He will then give me a good place in a cathedral. You shall not see me going about any more in a worn-out cassock. I shall have plenty of money, and I shall be able to help you and all your poor neighbors."

"But if the Pope dies?" asked Signora Concenza breathlessly.

"If the Pope dies, then no one can know — If my parish priest does n't happen to be in favor with his successor, we must both remain where we now are for many years to come."

Signora Concenza came close to her son and regarded him anxiously. She looked at his brow, which was covered with wrinkles, and at his hair that was just turning gray. He looked tired and worn. It was actually imperative that he should have that place at the cathedral right away. "To-night I shall go to church and pray for the Pope," thought she. "It won't do for him to die."

After supper she bravely conquered her fatigue and went out on the streets. Great crowds of people thronged there. Many were only curious and had gone out because they wished to catch the news of the death at first hand; but many were really distressed and wandered from church to church to pray.

As soon as Signora Concenza had come out on the street, she met one of her daughters, who was married to a lithographer. "Oh, mother, but you do right to come out and pray for him!" exclaimed the daughter. "You can't imagine what a misfortune it would be if he were to die! My Fabiano was ready to take his own life when he learned that the Pope was ill."

She related how her husband, the lithographer, had but just struck off hundreds of thousands of the Pope's pictures. Now, if the Pope were to die, he would n't be able to sell half of them — no, not even a quarter of them. He would be ruined. Their entire fortune was at stake.

She rushed on to gather some fresh news, wherewith she might comfort her poor husband, who did not dare venture out, but sat at home and brooded over his misfortune. Her mother stood still on the street, mumbling to herself: "It won't do for him to die. It will never do for him to die!"

She walked into the first church she came to. There she fell upon her knees and prayed for the life of the Pope.

As she arose to leave, she happened to lift her eyes to a little votive tablet which hung on the wall just above her head. The tablet was a representation of Death raising a terrifying two-edged sword to mow down a young girl, while her mother, who had cast herself in his path, tries in vain to receive the blow in place of her child.

She stood long before the picture, musing. "Signor Death is a careful arithmetician," she remarked. "One has never heard of his agreeing to exchange an old person for a young one."

She remembered her son's words that he would

be willing to die in the Pope's stead, and a shudder passed through her whole body. "Think, if Death were to take him at his word!"

"No, no, Signor Death!" she whispered. "You must n't believe him. You must understand that he did n't mean what he said. He wants to live. He does n't want to leave his old mother, who loves him."

For the first time the thought struck her that if any one should sacrifice himself for the Pope, it were better that she did it — she, who was already old and had lived her life.

When she left the church, she happened into the company of some nuns of the saintliest and most devout appearance, who lived in the northern part of the country. They had travelled down to Rome to obtain a little help from the Pope's treasury. "We are actually in the most dire need of aid," they told old Concenza. "Only think! our convent was so old and dilapidated that it blew down during the severe storm of last winter.. We may not now present our case to him. If he should die, we must return home with an unaccomplished mission. Who can know if his successor will be the sort of man who will trouble himself to succor poor nuns?"

It seemed as if all the people were thinking

the same thoughts. It was very easy to get into converse with any one. Each and all whom Signora Concenza approached let her know that the Pope's death would be for them a terrible misfortune.

The old woman repeated again and again to herself: "My son is right. It will never do for the Pope to die."

A nurse was standing among a group of people, talking in a loud voice. She was so affected that the tears streamed down her cheeks. She related how five years ago she had been ordered away, to serve at a leper hospital on an island at the other end of the globe. Naturally, she had to obey orders; but she did so against her wishes. She had felt a horrible dread of this mission. Before she left Rome, she was received by the Pope, who had given her a special blessing and had also promised her that if she came back alive she should have another audience with him. And it was upon this that she had lived during the five years she had been away — only on the hope that she might see the Holy Father once more in this life! This had helped her to go through all the horrors. And now, when she had got home at last, she was met by the news that he lay upon his death-bed! She could not even see him!

She was in extreme despair, and old Concenza was deeply moved. "It would really be much too great a sorrow for every one if the Pope were to die," thought she, as she wandered farther up the street.

When she observed that many of the passers-by looked perfectly exhausted from weeping, she thought with a sense of relief: "What a joy it would be to see everybody's happiness if the Pope should recover!" And she, like many others who have a buoyant disposition, was apparently no more afraid of dying than of living; so she said to herself: "If I only knew how it could be done, I would gladly give the Holy Father the years that are left to me of life."

She said this somewhat in jest, but back of the words there was also seriousness. She truly wished that she might realize something in that way. "An old woman could not wish for a more beautiful death," thought she. "I would be helping both my son and my daughter, and, besides, I should make great masses of people happy."

Just as this thought stirred within her, she raised the patched curtain which hung before the entrance of a gloomy little church. It was one of the very old churches — one of those which appear to be gradually sinking into the

earth because the city's foundation has, in the
intervening years, raised itself several metres all
around them. This church in its interior had
preserved somewhat of its ancient gloom, which
must have come down through the dark ages
during which it had sprung into existence. In-
voluntarily a shudder passed through one as one
stepped in under its low arches, which rested
upon uncommonly thick pillars, and saw the
crudely painted saints' pictures that glimpsed
down at one from walls and altars.

When Signora Concenza came into this old
church, which was thronged with worshippers,
she was seized with a mysterious awe and reverence. She felt that in this sanctuary there
verily lived a Deity. Beneath the massive
arches hovered something infinitely mighty and
mysterious, something which inspired such a
sense of annihilating superiority that she felt
nervous about remaining in there. "Ah, this is
no church where one goes to hear a mass or to
confessional," remarked Signora Concenza to
herself. "Here one comes when one is in great
trouble, when one can be helped in no other
way than through a miracle."

She lingered down by the door and breathed
in this strange air of mystery and gloom. "I
don't even know to whom this old church is

dedicated; but I feel that here there must be some one who is able to grant us that which we pray for."

She sank down among the kneeling people, who were so many that they covered the floor from the altar to the door. All the while that she herself was praying, she heard around her sighs and sobs. All this grief went to her heart and filled it with greater and greater compassion. "Oh, my God, let me do something to save the old man!" she prayed. "In the first place, I ought to help my children, and then all the other people."

Every once in a while a thin little monk stole in among the praying and whispered something in their ears. The one to whom he was speaking instantly stood up and followed him into the sacristy.

Signora Concenza soon apprehended what there was in question. "They are of the kind who give pledges for the Pope's recovery," thought she.

The next time the little monk made his rounds, she rose up and went with him. It was a perfectly involuntary action. She fancied that she was being impelled to do this by the power which ruled in the old church.

As soon as she came into the sacristy, which

was even more archaic and more mystical than
the church itself, she regretted it. "What have
I to do in here?" she asked herself. "What
have I to give away? I own nothing but a
couple of cartloads of garden truck. I certainly
can't present the saints with a few baskets of
artichokes!"

At one side of the room there was a long table
at which a priest stood recording in a register all
that was pledged to the saints. Concenza heard
how one promised to present the old church with
a sum of money, while a second promised to give
his gold watch, and a third her pearl earrings.

Concenza stood all the while down by the
door. Her last poor copper had been spent to
procure a few delicacies for her son. She saw a
number of persons who appeared to be no richer
than herself buying wax candles and silver hearts.
She turned her skirt pocket inside out, but she
could not afford even that much.

She stood and waited so long that finally she
was the only stranger in the sacristy. The
priests walking about in there looked at her a
little astonished. Then she took a step or two
forward. She seemed at the start uncertain and
embarrassed, but after the first move she
walked lightly and briskly up to the table.
"Your Reverence!" she said to the priest,

"write that Concenza Zamponi, who was sixty last year, on Saint John the Baptist's Day, gives all her remaining years to the Pope, that the thread of his life may be lengthened!"

The priest had already begun writing. He was probably very tired after having worked at this register the whole night, and thought no more about the sort of things he was recording. But now he stopped short in the middle of a word and looked quizzically at Signora Concenza. She met his glance very calmly.

"I am strong and well, your Reverence," said she. "I should probably have lived out my allotted seventy years. It is at least ten years that I am giving to the Holy Father."

The priest marked her zeal and reverence and offered no objections. "She is a poor woman," thought he. "She has nothing else to give."

"It is written, my daughter," he said.

When old Concenza came out from the church, it was so late that the commotion had ceased and the streets were absolutely deserted. She found herself in a remote part of the city, where the gas lamps were so far apart that they dispelled only a very little of the darkness. All the same, she walked on briskly. She felt very solemn within and was certain that she had done something which would make many people happy.

As she walked up the street, she suddenly got the impression that a live being circled above her head. In the darkness, between the tall houses, she thought she could distinguish a pair of large wings, and she even fancied she heard the sound of their beating.

"What is this?" said she. "Surely it can't be a bird! It is much too big for that." All at once she thought she saw a face which was so white that it illuminated the darkness. Then an unspeakable terror seized her. "It is the Angel of Death hovering over me," thought she. "Ah, what have I done? I have placed myself in the dreaded one's power!"

She started to run, but she could hear the rustle of the strong wings and was convinced that Death was pursuing her.

She fled with breathless haste through several streets, thinking all the while that Death was coming nearer and nearer her. She already felt his wings brushing against her shoulder.

Suddenly she heard a whizzing in the air, and something heavy and sharp struck her head. Death's two-edged sword had reached her. She sank to her knees. She knew that she must lose her life.

A few hours later, old Concenza was found on the street by two workmen. She lay there unconscious, stricken with apoplexy. The poor woman was immediately removed to a hospital, where they succeeded in bringing her to, but it was apparent that she could not live very long.

There was time, at all events, to send for her children. When, in a state of despair, they reached her sick-bed, they found her very calm and happy. She could n't speak many words to them, but she lay and caressed their hands. "You must be happy," said she, "happy, happy!" Evidently she did not like their crying. She also bade the nurses smile and show their joy. "Cheerful and happy," said she; "now you must be cheerful and happy!" She lay there with hunger in her eyes, waiting to see a little joy in their faces.

She grew more and more impatient with her children's tears and with the solemn faces of the nurses. She began to utter things which no one could comprehend. She said that in case they were not glad she might just as well have lived. Those who heard her thought she was raving.

Suddenly the doors opened, and a young physician came into the sick-room. He was waving a newspaper and calling in a loud voice:

"The Pope is better. He will live. A change has taken place in the night."

The nurses silenced him, so that he should n't disturb the dying woman, but Signora Concenza had already heard him.

She had also marked a spark of joy — a gleam of happiness which could not be concealed — pass through those who stood around her bed.

There she lay looking about her, with something far-seeing in her gaze. It was as though she were looking out over Rome, where the people were now thronging up and down the streets and greeting one another with the joyful news.

She raised her head as high as she could and said: "So am I — I am very happy. God has allowed me to die that he may live. I don't mind dying when I have made so many people happy."

She lay down again, and a few seconds later she was dead.

But they say in Rome that, after his recovery, the Holy Father entertained himself one day by looking through the church records of pious pledges which had been offered for his recovery.

Smilingly he read the long lists of little gifts until he came to the record where Concenza Zamponi had presented him with her remaining years of life. Instantly he became very serious and thoughtful.

He made inquiries about Concenza Zamponi and learned that she had died on the night of his recovery. He then bade them call to him her son, Dominico, and questioned him minutely as to her last moments.

"My son," said the Pope to him when he had spoken, "your mother has not saved my life, as she believed in her last hour; but I am deeply moved by her love and self-sacrifice."

He let Dominico kiss his hand, whereupon he dismissed him.

But the Romans assure you that, although the Pope would not admit that his span of years had been lengthened by the poor woman's gift, he was nevertheless certain of it. "Why else should Father Zamponi have had such a meteoric career?" asked the Romans. "He is already a bishop and it is whispered that he will soon be a Cardinal."

And in Rome they never feared after that that the Pope would die, not even when he was mortally ill. They were prepared to have him live longer than other people. His life had of course been lengthened by all the years that poor Concenza had given him.

The Story of a Story

The Story of a Story

ONCE there was a story that wanted to be told and sent out in the world. This was very natural, inasmuch as it knew that it was already as good as finished. Many, through remarkable deeds and strange events, had helped create it; others had added their straws in it by again and again relating these things. What it lacked was merely a matter of being joined together, so that it could travel comfortably through the country. As yet it was only a confused jumble of stories — a big, formless cloud of adventures rushing hither and thither like a swarm of stray bees on a summer's day, not knowing where they will find some one who can gather them into a hive.

The story that wanted to be told had sprung up in Vermland, and you may be sure that it circled over many mills and manors, over many parsonages and many homes of military officers, in the beautiful province, peering through the windows and begging to be cared for. But it was forced to make many futile attempts, for everywhere it was turned away. Anything else was

hardly to be expected. People had many things
of much more importance to think of.

Finally the story came to an old place called
Mårbacka. It was a little homestead, with low
buildings overshadowed by giant trees. At one
time it had been a parsonage, and it was as if
this had set a certain stamp upon the place
which it could not lose. They seemed to have a
greater love for books and reading there than
elsewhere, and a certain air of restfulness and
peace always pervaded it. There rushing with
duties and bickering with servants were never
met with, nor was hatred or dissension given
house room, either. One who happened to be a
guest there was not allowed to take life too
seriously, but had to feel that his first duty was to
be light-hearted and believe that for one and all
who lived on this estate our Lord managed everything for the best.

As I think of the matter now, I apprehend
that the story of which I am speaking must have
lingered thereabouts a great many years during
its vain longing to be told. It seems to me as
though it must have enwrapped the place, as
a mist shrouds a mountain summit, now and
then letting one of the adventures of which it
consisted rain down upon it.

They came in the form of strange ghost stories

about the superintendent of the foundries, who always had black bulls hitched to his wagon when he drove home at night from a revel. And in his home the Evil One himself used to sit in the rocker and rock while the wife sat at the piano and played. They came as true stories from the neighboring homestead, where crows had persecuted the mistress until she did n't dare venture outside the door; from the Captain's house, where they were so poor that everything had to be borrowed; from the little cottage down by the church, where there lived a lot of young and old girls who had all fallen in love with the handsome organ builder.

Sometimes the dear adventures came to the homestead in an even more tangible form. Aged and poverty-stricken army officers would drive up to the doorstep behind rickety old horses and in rickety carryalls. They would stop and visit for weeks, and in the evenings, when the toddy had put courage into them, they would talk of the time when they had danced in stockingless shoes, so that their feet would look small, of how they had curled their hair and dyed their mustaches. One of them told how he had tried to take a pretty young girl back to her sweetheart and how he had been hunted by wolves on the way; another had been at the Christmas feast where an angered guest had flung all the hazel-hens at the wall because some one had made him believe they were crows; a third had seen the old gentleman who used to sit at a plain board table and play Beethoven.

But the story could reveal its presence in still another way. In the attic hung the portrait of a lady with powdered hair, and when any one walked past it he was reminded that it was a portrait of the beautiful daughter of the Count, who had loved her brother's young tutor, and had called to see him once when she was an old gray-haired lady and he an old married man. In the lumber room were heaped up bundles of documents containing deeds of purchase and leases signed by the great lady, who once ruled over seven foundries which had been willed to her by her lover. If one entered the church, one saw in a dusty little cabinet under the pul-pit the chest filled with infidel manuscripts, which was not to be opened until the beginning of the new century. And not very far from the church is the river, at the bottom of which rests a pile of sacred images that were not allowed to remain in the pulpit and chancel they once had ornamented.

It must have been because so many legends and traditions hovered around the farm that one of the children growing up there longed to become a narrator. It was not one of the boys. They were not at home very much, for they were away at their schools almost the whole year; so the story did not get much of a hold upon them. But it was one of the girls — one who was delicate and could not romp and play like other children, but found her greatest enjoyment in reading and hearing stories about all the great and wonderful things which had happened in the world.

However, at the start it was not the girl's intention to write about the stories and legends surrounding her. She had n't the remotest idea that a book could be made of these adventures, which she had so often heard related that to her they seemed the most commonplace things in the world. When she tried to write, she chose material from her books, and with fresh courage she strung together stories of the Sultans in "Thousand and One Nights," Walter Scott's heroes, and Snorre Sturleson's "Kings of Romance."

Surely it is needless to state that what she wrote was the least original and the crudest that has ever been put upon paper. But this very naturally she herself did not see. She went about at home on the quiet farm, filling every scrap of paper she could lay her hands on with verse and prose, with plays and romances. When she was n't writing, she sat and waited for success. And success was to consist in this: Some stranger who was very learned and influential, through some rare freak of fortune, was to come and discover what she had written and find it worth printing. After that, all the rest would come of itself.

Meanwhile nothing of the sort happened. And when the girl had passed her twentieth year, she began to grow impatient. She wondered why success did not come her way. Perhaps she lacked knowledge. She probably needed to see a little more of the world than the homestead in Vermland. And seeing that it would be a long time before she could earn her livelihood as an author, it was necessary for her to learn something — find some work in life — that she might have bread while she waited for herself. Or maybe it was simply this — that the story had lost patience with her. Perhaps it thought thus: "Since this blind person does not see that which lies nearest her eyes, let her be forced to go away. Let her tramp upon gray stone streets; let her live in cramped city rooms with no other outlook than gray stone walls; let her live among people who hide everything that is unusual in them and who appear to be all alike. It may perchance teach her to see that which is waiting outside the gate of her home — all that lives and moves between the stretch of blue hills which she has every day before her eyes."

And so, one autumn, when she was two-and-twenty, she travelled up to Stockholm to begin preparing herself for the vocation of teacher.

The girl soon became absorbed in her work. She wrote no more, but went in for studies and lectures. It actually looked as though the story would lose her altogether.

Then something extraordinary happened. This same autumn, after she had been living a couple of months amidst gray streets and house walls, she was walking one day up Malmskillnad Street with a bundle of books under her arm. She had just come from a lecture on the history of literature. The lecture must have been about Bellman and Runeberg, because she was thinking of them and of the characters that live in their verses. She said to herself that Runeberg's jolly warriors and Bellman's happy-go-lucky roisterers were the very best material a writer could have to work with. And suddenly this thought flashed upon her: Vermland, the world in which you have been living, is not less re-

markable than that of Fredman or Fänrik Stål.
If you can only learn how to handle it, you will
find that your material is quite as good as theirs.

This is how it happened that she caught her
first glimpse of the story. And the instant she
saw it, the ground under her seemed to sway.
The whole long Malmskillnad Street from Hamn
Street Hill to the fire-house rose toward the skies
and sank again — rose and sank. She stood
still a long while, until the street had settled
itself. She gazed with astonishment at the
passers-by, who walked calmly along, apparently
oblivious to the miracle that had taken place.

At that moment the girl determined that she
would write the story of Vermland's Cavaliers,
and never for an instant did she relinquish the
thought of it; but many and long years elapsed
before the determination was carried out.

In the first place she had entered upon a new
field of labor, and she lacked the time needful
for the carrying out of a great literary work.
In the second place she had failed utterly in her
first attempts to write the story.

During these years many things were constantly happening which helped mould it. One
morning, on a school holiday, she was sitting
at the breakfast-table with her father, and the
two of them talked of old times. Then he began

telling of an acquaintance of his youth, whom
he described as the most fascinating of men.
This man brought joy and cheer with him wherever he went. He could sing; he composed music;
he improvised verse. If he struck up a dance,
it was not alone the young folk who danced,
but old men and old women, high and low. If
he made a speech, one had to laugh or cry,
whichever he wished. If he drank himself full,
he could play and talk better than when he was
sober, and when he fell in love with a woman, it
was impossible for her to resist him. If he did
foolish things, one forgave him; if he was sad at
times, one wanted to do anything and everything to see him glad again. But any great
success in life he had never had, despite his
wealth of talents. He had lived mostly at the
foundries in Vermland as private tutor. Finally
he was ordained as a minister. This was the
highest that he had attained.

After this conversation she could see the hero
of her story better than heretofore, and with
this a little life and action came into it. One
fine day a name was given to the hero and he was
called Gösta Berling. Whence he got the name
she never knew. It was as if he had named
himself.

Another time, she came home to spend the

Christmas holidays. One evening the whole family went off to a Christmas party a good distance from home in a terrible blizzard. It turned out to be a longer drive than one would have thought. The horse ploughed his way ahead at a walking pace. For several hours she sat there in the sleigh in the blinding snowstorm and thought of the story. When they arrived finally, she had thought out her first chapter. It was the one about the Christmas night at the smithy.

What a chapter! It was her first and for many years her only one. It was first written in verse, for the original plan was that it should be a romance cycle, like "Fänrik Stål's Sagas." But by degrees this was changed, and for a time the idea was that it should be written as drama. Then the Christmas night was worked over to go in as the first act. But this attempt did not succeed, either; at last she decided to write the story as a novel. Then the chapter was written in prose. It grew enormously long, covering forty written pages. The last time it was rewritten it took up only nine.

After a few more years came a second chapter. It was the story of the Ball at Borg and of the wolves that hunted Gösta Berling and Anna Stjernhök.

In the beginning this chapter was not written with the thought that it could come into the story, but as a sort of chance composition to be read at a small social gathering. The reading, however, was postponed, and the novelette was sent to *Dagny*. After a time the story was returned as unavailable for the magazine. It was in reality not available anywhere. As yet it was altogether lacking in artistic smoothness.

Meanwhile the author wondered to what purpose this unluckily born novelette could be turned. Should she put it into the story? To be sure, it was an adventure by itself — and ended. It would look odd among the rest, which were better connected. Perhaps it would n't be such a bad idea, she thought then, if all the chapters of the story were like this one — almost finished adventures? This would be difficult to carry out, but it might possibly be done. There would doubtless be gaps in the continuity here and there, but that should give to the book great strength and variety.

Now two important matters were settled: The story was to be a novel, and each chapter should be complete in itself. But nothing much had been gained hereby. She who had been fired with the idea of writing the story of Vermland's Cavaliers when she was two-and-twenty, at this stage was nearing the thirties and had not been able to write more than two chapters. Where had the years gone? She had been graduated from the Teachers' College and for several years past had been a teacher at Landskrona. She had become interested in much and had been occupied with many things, but the story was just as unwritten. A mass of material had certainly been collected, but why was it so hard for her to write it down? Why did the inspiration never come to her? Why did the pen glide so slowly over the paper? She certainly had her dark moments at that time! She began to think that she never would finish her novel. She was that servant who buried his talent in the ground and never tried to use it.

As a matter of fact, all this occurred during the eighties, when stern Realism was at its height. She admired the great masters of that time, never thinking that one could use any other style in writing than the one they employed. For her own part, she liked the Romanticists better, but Romanticism was dead, and she was hardly the one to think of reviving its form and expression! Although her brain was filled to overflowing with stories of ghosts and mad love, of wondrously beautiful women and adventure-loving cavaliers, she tried to write about it in calm, realistic prose. She was not very clear-visioned. Another would have seen that the impossible was impossible.

Once she wrote a couple of chapters in another style. One was a scene from Svartsjö churchyard; the other was about the old philosopher, Uncle Eberhard, and his infidel manuscripts. She scribbled them mostly in fun, with many ohs and ahs in the prose, which made it almost rhythmical. She perceived that in this vein she could write. There was inspiration in this — she could feel it. But when the two short chapters were finished, she laid them aside. They were only written in fun. One could not write a whole book in that vein.

But now the story had been waiting long enough. It thought, no doubt, as it did at the time when it sent her out in the world: "Again I must send this blinded person a great longing which will open her eyes."

The longing came over her in this manner: The homestead where she had grown up was sold. She journeyed to the home of her childhood to see it once again before strangers should occupy it.

The evening before she left there, perhaps nevermore to see the dear old place, she concluded in all meekness and humility to write the book in her own way and according to her own poor abilities. It was not going to be any great masterwork, as she had hoped. It might be a book at which people would laugh, but anyway she would write it — write it for herself, to save for herself what she could still save of the home — the dear old stories, the sweet peace of the care-free days, and the beautiful landscape with the long lakes and the many-hued blue hills.

But for her, who had hoped that she might yet learn to write a book people would care to read, it seemed as though she had relinquished the very thing in life she had been most eager to win. It was the hardest sacrifice she had made thus far.

A few weeks later, she was again at her home in Landskrona, seated at her writing-desk. She began writing — she did n't know exactly what it was to be — but she was not going to be afraid of the strong words, the exclamations, the interrogations, nor would she be afraid to give herself with all her childishness and all her dreams! After she had come to this decision, the pen began to move almost by itself. This made her quite delirious. She was carried away with enthusiasm. Ah, this was writing! Unfamiliar thoughts and things, or, rather, things

she never had surmised were stored away in her
brain, crowded down upon the paper. The
pages were filled with a haste of which she had
never dreamed. What had hitherto required
months — no, years — to work out, was now
accomplished in a couple of hours. That evening she wrote the story of the young countess'
tramp over the ice on River Löven, and the
flood at Ekeby.

The following afternoon she wrote the scene
in which the gouty ensign, Rutger von Örneclou,
tries to raise himself in bed to dance the Cachuca,
and the evening of the next day appeared the
story of the old *Mamsell* who went off to visit
thè parsimonious Broby clergyman.

Now she knew for certain that in this style
she could write the book; but she was just as
certain that no one would have the patience to
read it through.

However, not many chapters let themselves
be written like this — in one breath. Most of
them required long and arduous labor, and there
were only little snatches of time in the after-
noons which she could devote to authorship.
When she had been writing about half a year,
reckoning from the day when she had gone
in for romanticism with a vengeance, about
a dozen chapters were written. At this rate

the book would be finished in three or four years.

It was in the spring of this year, 1890, that *Idun* invited prize competitors to send in short novelettes of about one hundred printed pages. This was an outlet for a story that wanted to be told and sent into the world. It must have been the story itself that prompted her sister to suggest to her that she make use of this opportunity. Here, at last, was a way of finding out if her story was so hopelessly bad! If it received the prize, much would be gained; if it did n't, she simply stood in exactly the same position as before.

She had nothing against the idea, but she had so little faith in herself that she could n't come to any conclusion.

Finally, just eight days before the time for submitting manuscripts had expired, she decided to take from the novel five chapters which were sufficiently well connected to pass for a novelette, and chance it with these. But the chapters were far from ready. Three of them were loosely written, but of the remaining two there was barely an outline. Then the whole thing must be legibly copied, of course. To add to this, she was not at home just then, but was visiting her sister and brother-in-law, who still lived in Vermland. And one who has come to visit with dear friends for a short time cannot spend the days at a writing-desk. She wrote therefore at night, sitting up the whole week until four in the mornings.

Finally there were only twenty-four hours of the precious time left, and there were still twenty pages to be written.

On this the last day they were invited out. The whole family were going on a little journey to be gone for the night. Naturally, she had to accompany the rest. When the party was over and the guests dispersed, she sat up all night writing in the strange place.

At times she felt very queer. The place where she was visiting was the very estate on which the wicked Sintram had lived. Fate, in a singular way, had brought her there on the very night when she must write about him who sat in the rocker and rocked.

Now and then she looked up from her work and listened in the direction of the drawing-room for the possible sound of a pair of rockers in motion. But nothing was heard. When the clock struck six the next morning, the five chapters were finished.

Along in the forenoon they travelled home on a little freight steamer. There her sister did up the parcel, sealed it with sealing-wax, which had been brought from home for this purpose, wrote the address, and sent off the novelette.

This happened on one of the last days in July. Toward the end of August *Idun* contained a notice to the effect that something over twenty manuscripts had been received by the editors, but that one or two among them were so confusedly written they could not be counted in.

Then she gave up waiting for results. She knew, of course, which novelette was so confusedly written that it could not be counted in.

One afternoon in November she received a curious telegram. It contained simply the words "Hearty Congratulations," and was signed by three of her college classmates.

For her it was a terribly long wait until dinner-time of the following day, when the Stockholm papers were distributed. When the paper was in her hands, she had to search long without finding anything. Finally, on the last page she found a little notice in fine print which told that the prize had been awarded to her.

To another it might not have meant so much, perhaps, but for her it meant that she could devote herself to the calling which all her life she had longed to follow.

There is but little to add to this: The story that wanted to be told and sent out in the world was now fairly near its destination. Now it was to be written, at least, even though it might take a few years more before it was finished.

She who was writing it had gone up to Stockholm around Christmas time, after she had received the prize.

The editor of *Idun* volunteered to print the book as soon as it was finished.

If she could ever find time to write it!

The evening before she was to return to Landskrona, she spent with her loyal friend, Baroness Adlersparre,[1] to whom she read a few chapters aloud.

"Esselde" listened, as only she could listen, and she became interested. After the reading she sat silently and pondered. "How long will it be before all of it is ready?" she asked finally.

"Three or four years."

Then they parted.

The next morning, two hours before she was to leave Stockholm, a message came from

---

[1] Baroness Adlersparre — pen name, Esselde — was a noted Swedish writer, publisher, and philanthropist, and a contemporary of Fredrika Bremer.

Esselde bidding her come to her before the departure.

The old Baroness was in her most positive and determined mood. "Now you must take a leave of absence for a year and finish the book. I shall procure the money."

Fifteen minutes later the girl was on her way to the Principal of the Teachers' College to ask her assistance in securing a substitute.

At one o'clock she was happily seated in the railway carriage. But now she was going no farther than Sörmland, where she had good friends who lived in a charming villa.

And so they — Otto Gumaelius and his wife — gave her the freedom of their home — freedom to work, and peace, and the best of care for nearly a year, until the book was finished.

Now, at last, she could write from morning till night. It was the happiest time of her life.

But when the story was finished at the close of the summer, it looked queer. It was wild and disordered, and the connecting threads were so loose that all the parts seemed bent upon following their old inclination to wander off, each in its own way.

It never became what it should have been.

CPSIA information can be obtained at www.ICGtesting.com
Printed in the USA
LVOW01s1815040215

425712LV00027B/798/P